Stand

Gary T. Hartfield

Published by Richter Publishing LLC
http://www.richterpublishing.com

Book formatted by: Casey Cavanagh

Book Cover Designed by: Roman Galisevych

ISBN:0692549579

ISBN-13:9780692549575

DISCLAIMER

This book is designed to provide information on entrepreneurship only. This information is provided and sold with the knowledge that the publisher and author do not offer any legal or medical advice. In the case of a need for any such expertise consult with the appropriate professional. This book does not contain all information available on the subject. This book has not been created to be specific to any individual people or organizations' situation or needs. Reasonable efforts have been made to make this book as accurate as possible. However, there may be typographical and or content errors. Therefore, this book should serve only as a general guide and not as the ultimate source of subject information. This book contains information that might be dated or erroneous and is intended only to educate and entertain. The author and publisher shall have no liability or responsibility to any person or entity regarding any loss or damage incurred, or alleged to have incurred, directly or indirectly, by the information contained in this book or as a result of anyone acting or failing to act upon the information in this book. You hereby agree never to sue and to hold the author and publisher harmless from any and all claims arising out of the information contained in this book. You hereby agree to be bound by this disclaimer, covenant not to sue and release. You may return this book within the guarantee time period for a full refund. In the interest of full disclosure, if this book contains any affiliate links they might pay the author or publisher a commission upon any purchase from the company. While the author and publisher take no responsibility for any virus or technical issues that could be

DEDICATION

This book is dedicated to my parents, Booketee W. Hartfield Sr. and Norma J. Hartfield, who have encouraged and supported me throughout my life's experiences.

I also dedicate this book to my children: Ashley, Imani and Garrett. You are my inspiration.

CONTENTS

ACKNOWLEDGMENTS

I extend grateful acknowledgement to everyone who contributed to the book, including Valerie Goddard, Aunt Tukie, Tony Jenkins, Dr. Thomas Reuschling, Austin "Bud" Llewlyn, Frank Gemma and John Snell.

To my cousin, Kebra Bunkley, thank you for the art-work illustration of Jacob wrestling with the angel of God. You are truly gifted.

To my writing coach, Dr. Vernetta Williams, you are the best. Thank you for pushing and guiding me throughout this process.

FOREWORD

On this journey called life, special people we encounter make our life rich and full of meaning. Rarely do we meet someone and as a result of that encounter, our life and its trajectory are forever changed. I had that life-changing encounter one day in an elevator. Since that time, I've had the pleasure of having a front row seat on the journey to success of Gary T Hartfield.

Throughout my collegiate experiences and professional career with the Department of Defense and as a non-profit executive, I have encountered many strong and effective leaders in the for-profit, non-profit and government arenas. Rarely have I encountered powerful leaders who were also strong in character, committed to their values, willing to share their successes and their challenges and offer support to others.

Several men and women, who are professors, CEO's and clergy, have inspired and challenged me to expand my vision and work to make a greater impact on the communities in which I lived. These mentors have shaped my career path and ministry and inspired me to devote my life to maximizing potential in people, organizations and communities.

I have personally witnessed Gary's untiring

commitment and support as he stood with me while we worked to achieve a goal when the odds were stacked against us. We decided to enter the race for County Commission in 2010. We were the proverbial "underdog" and not thought of as a serious candidate. Gary stood with me through every twist and turn of the campaign. From walking precincts in the scorching heat, attending events, preparing for debates and withstanding erroneous stories, Gary stood strong! He stood strong when even I had moments of doubt.

Gary's leadership in the campaign came from his never tiring work ethic, analytical insight, personal investment, true grit and "can do attitude." Gary was relentless and said, "We will not give up or give in. We will work until the end." We did not win the election; however, we won OUR campaign and surprised everyone by beating the incumbent.

More importantly, we successfully demonstrated that we could hold fast to our values, serve our constituency and communicate our platform in a manner that was received by people from all walks of life and both sides of the political spectrum.

This is just one example of Gary standing strong in the midst of overwhelming odds. His life is a testament to perseverance. I have witnessed Gary overcome obstacles that would have sidetracked many people; instead, Gary reached up to heaven and looked inward to gain renewed strength, wisdom and guidance which

2

have propelled him forward toward his divine destiny.

Coming from humble beginnings, Gary had a vision far greater than his small town. He placed his vision in the Master's hand and, step by step, that vision has grown into something great! From Defuniak Springs to the board room of Fortune 500 companies, Gary has worked diligently to achieve great personal and entrepreneurial success. He is now focusing his attention on expanding his business ventures so that he can create a legacy of success and wealth for his family and the next generation.

Gary Hartfield is a phenomenal man whose success and strength are anchored in his faith and trust in God as well as his ability to remain humble and grateful for all of his blessings. His journey to success is remarkable and full of life-lessons.

As you read the pages of this book, you will discover life lessons to learn, business strategies to gain, wealth principles to be mastered and wisdom to receive as you prepare to stand strong to fulfill your dreams and visions. I invite you to "tap into" his wisdom as I have and allow him to mentor you as you chart your course and prepare yourself to embrace the fullness of abundance that is your divine destiny.

Valerie H. Goddard
CEO, The Goddard Group

INTRODUCTION

My "Journey to Success" required me to travel through three "zones" of life, a journey that draws many parallels to the children of Israel. The journey of the Israelites from Egypt to the Promised Land paints a powerful perspective of three distinct zones people live in regarding God's abundance. In one way or another, every person today is living in one of the three zones described below:

Egypt: the zone of "Never Enough." When the children of Israel lived in Egypt, they were slaves to cruel task masters and given only meager rations of food. In Egypt, people operate within a cruel system that is not intended to fully benefit them though they are doing a lot of work.

Wilderness: the zone of "Barely Enough." After being delivered from the bondage and scarce provisions of Egypt, the Israelites wandered for 40 years in the wilderness. Despite the failure of the children of Israel to consistently trust and obey the Lord, He met all their needs in the wilderness, but just barely. God provided manna for them to eat each day, but it couldn't be stored up nor were there leftovers. In the Wilderness, people survive but does not thrive.

The Promised Land (Canaan): the zone of "More

Than Enough." Though the Israelites probably got accustomed to their daily routine of gathering manna and having barely enough, God had much more planned for them in the Promised Land (Canaan). Scripture describes the Promised Land as an exceedingly good land that had huge crops and flows with milk and honey. People living in the Promised Land enjoy God's abundant provision.

The zones of "Egypt" and the "Wilderness" are safe zones. They represent the entitlement systems and safety net provided by being employed by someone. Many people are so afraid of risk that they spend their entire lives in Egypt, the land of "Not Enough." A few people are willing to venture out of this zone into the Wilderness, the zone of "Just Enough." However, both of these zones often rob people of our greatest moments and memories. God wants so much more for you; He wants you to leave the wilderness and enter the Promised Land, the land of "More Than Enough."

By a resolve to stand, I left my safe zones in order to enjoy God's blessing to the fullest. This memoir chronicles my journey through these three zones, through my eyes; it also includes perspectives of several witnesses to my journey at critical junctures. I share lessons and inspiration that helped me to progress along my journey. By recording my journey through these three zones, I hope to motivate you to start, continue and finish your journey to The Promised Land.

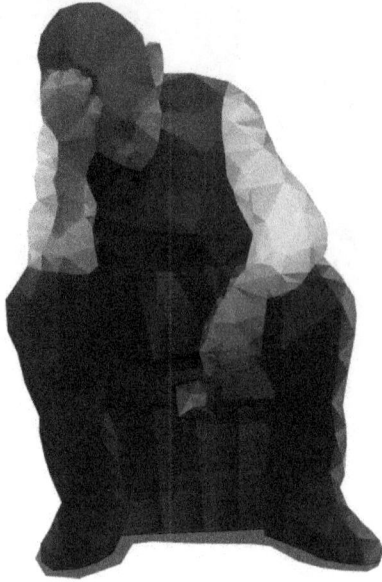

CHAPTER 1: CHRISTIAN BABY

"Before I formed you in the womb I knew you, before you were born I set you apart; I appointed you as a prophet to the nations." -Jeremiah 1:5

Born August 17, 1970, in Fort Walton Beach, Florida, I was given various nick-names by my family. However, my maternal grandmother, Irene Hunter-Goodson, gave me the one nickname that spoke my destiny: "Christian Baby."

I would love to say that my grandmother called me

"Christian Baby" because I was such a model child, but the opposite was true. Every time one of my siblings or cousins told my grandmother something bad that I had done, her response was, "No, not my Christian baby; he wouldn't do that," which often shamed me into behaving accordingly because I was, indeed, guilty.

As a child, I possessed the tendency to quit. I clearly remember my first year of little-league football and little-league baseball. Though I didn't like football, I played because it was "the" sport in my neighborhood; all the guys could be found on the football field. I vividly recall running, loaded down with all of the pads in the hot sun; in my little mind, I thought, "This is for the birds." Continually running into other players, hurting my teammates and hurting myself never made sense to me, so I quit nearly every other day.

Ironically, I was one of the best players on the team, and the field where we practiced wasn't far from my house. So, every time I quit, the coaches came to my house to encourage me to return. They saw something in me and always convinced me to rejoin the team. I was fairly good at football; however, I had no real connection to the team nor the sport. I played because it was the "in" thing to do, and I could play without exerting much effort.

My pattern of quitting and being persuaded to return to the team happened all the way to high school. Two things resulted from my back and forth dance with football. First, I had a consciousness at a young age that playing football was less about me and more about the coaches, who wanted to win at every level, whether in little league, high school or the pros. In my community, scouts were pervasive; they tracked kids from an early age. The second thing I developed was a mindset of expecting others to look for me and plead with me to keep going whenever I quit.

After some time, the coaches stopped trying to convince me to return to the team when I quit and began speaking to my mom. My mother was indifferent to me playing sports, but she was the parent who guided me in all areas of my life. My dad lived in Chicago working most of my childhood, so he had no direct influence on my growth and maturation as a young man or athlete.

My mother provided an educational, athletic and spiritual foundation for me. The spiritual foundation was probably the strongest of the three; I went to church with my mom, became familiar with scripture through my mom, knew the value of praying to seek guidance from God due to my mom and was exposed to Christmas and Easter speeches at church because of my mother.

Regarding football, I heard my mother tell my aunts and uncles about me quitting while I was outside playing marbles; she seemingly laughed it off. Nonetheless, my mother's authority caused me to return to the team, and I played football throughout high school. I was a member of the junior Varsity squad for the first few years. We had a fairly good team; in fact, our Varsity team won the State 2A championship in 1985.

My experiences in little league sports and continued involvement in athletics throughout the years reflect my middle class upbringing. My parents could afford to place and keep me in sports, regardless of how many times I quit, which exposed me to experiences and relationships beyond the athletic field I would not have had otherwise.

One of my fondest memories from little-league is camping for a weekend at Butch Abbott's farm. Most players spent the weekend on Butch Abbott's farm with his family. We fished, swam, hunted, rode horses and did almost everything else young men might want to experience on a farm, including throwing cow patties on each other. Thankfully, Butch Abbott's son, Shane, continues this tradition with some of the young athletes in the community today.

When spending time with my teammates on the field and away from the field, race did not matter to me or anyone else. We were simply young boys enjoying brotherhood and experiences I imagine most people would envy. Brotherhood and team work are two of the many great character builders I developed while playing organized sports throughout my upbringing.

Though I became a father to a beautiful baby girl named Ashley the week before I turned 16, my parents always expected me to attend college or a military academy. Therefore, I never considered anything other than obtaining a college degree after high school. The educational focus in my home caused me to research career options early. I took interest inventories and researched the projected job market because I was engaged in my future.

Based upon my research, I decided to be a Psychologist and earn a doctorate in Psychology. I chose this field because I always possessed a natural curiosity about the human mind and its workings. I often asked myself, "Why do people act differently? What behaviors are people born with and which ones are taught? What happens psychologically to young men and women during puberty?"

At 17, I was so clear about my career path that I was highly motivated to attend college. After discussing my career aspirations with my parents, my mother stated I should become an engineer. Because my mother had not graduated from high school at the time she gave me this advice, she had no earthly idea of the rigorous course work required to pursue an engineering degree. Nevertheless, my mother was the parent who had raised and guided me throughout the entire 17 years of my life; she was the person who provided a stable foundation for me and refused to allow me to quit; she was the parent whose guidance I had depended on all of my life, so I trusted and followed her advice.

After graduating from Walton Senior High in DeFuniak Springs, FL, in 1988, I journeyed to Florida Agricultural and Mechanical University (FAMU) in Tallahassee, the nation's largest Historically Black College or University (HBCU). I was completely oblivious to the numerous struggles that awaited me.

In the eyes of others...

My mother, Gary's grandmother, named Gary "Christian baby" because he was so bad as a little boy and had a bad temper. She started calling Gary a Christian to embarrass him into doing right; it was her way of shaming him into doing right and it worked because he would stop. Gary would not have temper tantrums around her.

From a child, Gary has always been sensitive. He named some chickens that his dad brought home to sell. One of them he named Fred; when Fred was dressed and killed, Gary cried. Another incident I recall is when Gary was about 4 years old; his sister, Tammy, cut bald spots in his hair. In order for his hair to grow back evenly, Gary had to get all of his hair shaved off; kids started calling him Kojak, and he was really sensitive about that name. Gary was quiet and didn't talk much, but when he opened his mouth, he had something to say. Gary has always been exceptional

In my home, I have a picture of Gary with the scripture 1 Chronicles 4:10 in it; the scripture is known as the prayer of Jabez. I see something in Gary and God's hand on him. Like Jabez prayed to God, I want God to enlarge Gary's territory and for God's hand to always be with him.

-Alice Hennessey, affectionately called "Aunt Tukie"

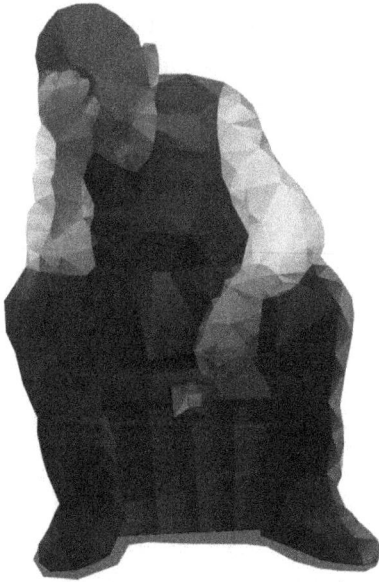

CHAPTER 2: THE NEGATIVE POWER OF INFLUENCE

"Think twice before you speak, because your words and influence will plant the seed of either success or failure in the mind of another." – Napoleon Hill

Unbeknownst to me, my mother's influence to switch my major from psychology to engineering would change my life forever. Upon my arrival to college, I attempted to register for every class that interested me, which was approximately 42 hours of varied classes in Nursing, Psychology and Sociology, among others. None of the classes I selected were engineering related.

After being misled and left to figure out this "registration thing," I found an advisor within the College of Engineering. Unfortunately, he wasn't much help. Though he advised me on the courses required for my major, he offered no insight on obtaining a full-time course load or guidance on the curriculum flow-chart for the major. I quickly lost confidence in the school's motto of "Excellence with Caring." After a degree of difficulty, I learned to register correctly and started my post-secondary educational journey.

However, I immediately faced an internal struggle as a college student because I was pursuing a major for which I lacked desire. As a result, I had to attend classes, read textbooks and complete assignments on information that did not interest me. The curriculum was challenging for those with a genuine passion to study engineering to the point that some had to change their majors, so imagine the difficulty I faced as someone interested in the mind and decision making!

I was forced to study subjects like advanced mathematics, physics, chemistry and other hard sciences. What intensified my frustration was knowing the person who had convinced me to pursue this major would never empathize with me. I could not explain to my mother the battle of trying to earn Cs in my classes so that I would not have to repeat them. I knew my mother would not understand the need for me to study for one class from 7:00 pm in the evening until 4:00 am in the morning and still not grasp the material. I knew she could not relate to me having to take a test with only two problems on it but needing four hours to complete the two questions. My angst was further exacerbated when I encountered those who grasped the concepts effortlessly while I struggled to comprehend information.

In addition to the internal turmoil I experienced, I encountered numerous external issues due to the bureaucracy inherent to a large state university; my enthusiasm as a first year college student quickly morphed into the overwhelming weariness of a first generation college student who lacked a knowledgeable support system.

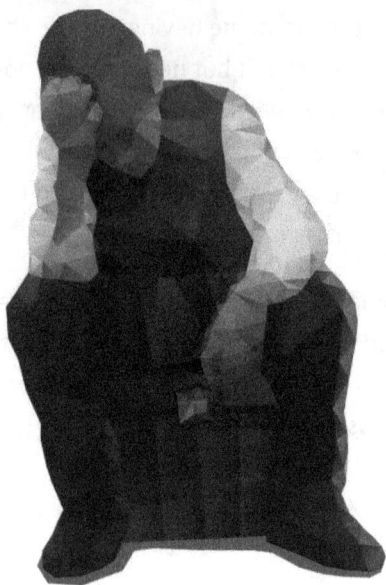

CHAPTER 3: A TIME TO STAND

"It's not whether you fall or make a mistake, it's what you do when you fall. I say to you, Stand Up. You keep Standing Up. It's not how many times you fall, it's how many times you STAND UP" —Cary-Hiroyuki Tagawa

After two semesters of course work, my persistent problems with college acclimation coupled with poor Student Affairs infrastructure engulfed me.

A significant part of my difficulty transitioning successfully to college was the lack of financial support.

Neither my parents nor I knew I needed my books early or at least on time to start classes. The nature of my engineering-based curriculum required costly supplemental items for my courses, such as lab materials, engineering paper, T-square, an architect scale and engineering calculator. My books and supplies easily totaled more than $500 per semester, which was in addition to tuition, rent, food, gas and other living expenses.

Though they were relatively middle class, my parents did not have the income to support these costs. Therefore, weeks passed before I obtained my books and supplies, causing me to fall behind in my courses from the beginning of each semester; consequently, my grades suffered. After some time, my ability to secure financial aid was suspended. Simply put, my grades were too low for me to qualify to receive financial-aid. This inability to obtain financial aid severely impacted my capacity to afford college expenses.

One day, I attempted to register for classes and couldn't because I had "holds." Before the contemporary conveniences of technology, automated systems and electronic processes, registering for classes at a university could be a nightmare. Resolving holds placed on a student's account became a living horror film at times.

At my undergraduate school, registration holds were primarily due to the poor student affairs' infrastructure at the University. Students had to wait in line for hours over a period of several days in order to speak with the proper personnel in the Financial Aid and/or Registrar's Office to discover the reason for a registration "hold." Generally, the holds were due to a University error, such as not having record that students had paid their deposit for housing. Consequently, the system placed students in a "Hold" status, and they could not register for classes. I witnessed several students crying in the registration lines that circled around the Grand Ballroom before finally giving up and returning home or transferring to another school.

Due to my registration holds, lack of financial resources, inability to secure financial aid, poor academic guidance and lack of general preparation for college, I quickly reached my breaking point. Not sure exactly the reasons for my registration hold, I left the Registrar's building, went to my car, drove off campus and started to cry. I stopped at a pay phone to call my mother collect and tell her about my horrendous experience.

The entire time I related my nightmare of being unable to register and having difficulty adjusting to college, I was thinking, "This is insurmountable! Once I explain to my mother that I have done everything possible, including what she has told me to do, I can return to the safety, security and familiarity of home. She will tell me, 'Ok, baby. Just pack up your things and come home.'"

As I vehemently explained that the situation could not be worked out, my mom said, "Gary, you know what I want you to do?" I thought my mom was going to give me some instructions; to which I could have easily replied, "I have already done that, mama." However, my mother said something unexpected, "Gary, I want you to STAND and after you have done everything possible... (*I still was thinking this was my ticket home*)... I want you to STAND ANYHOW!" While this was not the response I neither desired nor expected, it birthed my transition from a boy to a man.

I suddenly realized I could not revert to my childhood and adolescent years of quitting. Ironically, the same woman who had influenced me into the despicable major was now forcing me to persevere through the hardships. She was forcing me to return to the academic squad, just as she had done so many times with football.

At that very moment, all of my excuses were rendered invalid, so I had none to offer. Through my mom, I was given the immutable truth and greatest weapon of all to fight and STAND on God's Word. A seed of truth, based on Ephesians 6:10-18, part of which says *"and having done all, to stand. Stand therefore..."* was planted in my life for me to refer to again and again in order to gain the strength, persistence and motivation to continue life's journey, even until this day.

God knew my parents did not have the resources to sustain me. However, He gave my mother a word, the very thing He knew I needed to be brought into my destiny. I didn't need money, good grades, athletic scholarships or an easy ride; God set this moment up in order for me to need Him. What makes this moment so divine is that as life-transforming as this conversation was for me, my mother has no recollection of it. I truly believe God did not want her to be able to claim this moment. He wanted and desires the glory for the powerful words that forced me to stand and grow into a man.

Thank God for using my mother to speak LIFE into me. Indeed, the two words of "Stand Anyhow" spoken by my mother in that moment changed my life and the life of my off-spring, their off-spring and all with whom we come in contact.

The life altering words of "STAND ANYHOW" changed my life's legacy from victim to victor.

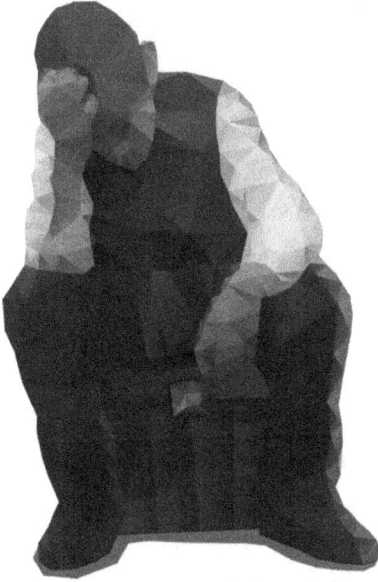

CHAPTER 4: LIGHTING A CANDLE

*"A candle loses nothing of its light by lighting
another candle" –James Keller*

Determined to heed my mother's advice to stand
and earn my bachelor's degree in Engineering, I
continued my tumultuous journey at FAMU. Sure
enough, I acquired some beneficial information through
my act of standing. One valuable lifetime skill was
gained during my first African-American History class,
which was taught by Attorney Williams. On the first day
of class, Attorney Williams reviewed the syllabus and
varied details of the class then gave the class an

assignment from the book, asking us to be prepared to discuss the assignment during our next meeting.

During the next class meeting, he realized that no one had read the book or prepared to discuss the topic. At that point, Attorney Williams uttered the most profound words in my ENTIRE undergraduate experience; he rhetorically asked, "Why are you waiting for someone else to educate you about your own damn History? I have heard you complain that some of your respective high schools didn't offer African American history and the most you learned was Harriet Tubman, the Underground Railroad and Dr. Martin Luther King Jr's "I have a Dream" speech. Here you have been given the opportunity to learn about your History and you will not take advantage of it; don't wait for someone else to educate you about your history!"

The words of Attorney Williams resonated in my soul. They awakened a thirst in me to learn more about my ancestors and our struggle. My newfound aggressive approach to my education caused Attorney Williams to affectionately refer to me as "Hell-Raiser." From that day, I always had something to say in class, and it usually was passionate. During one class meeting, I informed Attorney Williams and the class that the title of our book, *From Slavery to Freedom*, was incorrect because blacks in America still were not "free," declaring as former slave and abolitionist Frederick Douglas stated in a speech in 1886, "Where justice is denied, where poverty is enforced, where ignorance

23

prevails, and where any one class is made to feel that society is an organized conspiracy to oppress, rob and degrade them, neither persons nor property will be safe."

Attorney Williams changed my perspective about education and life. Until that point, like many of my classmates, I had taken education for granted; for us, it was simply a necessary means to obtaining the desired end of getting a college degree. I was not excited about my courses, school or learning. I expected professors to educate me on what I needed to know. However, the words of Attorney Williams challenged me to take responsibility for my learning and destiny. He taught me that if I needed to know or obtain something, then I should research it and acquire it myself. Throughout my life, I have applied this lesson to everything, not just history or education. Rest in Peace Attorney Williams.

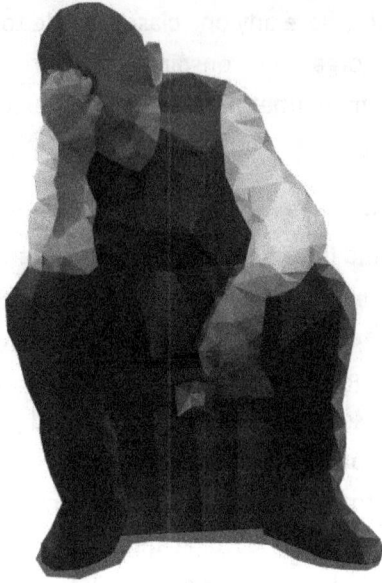

CHAPTER 5: PAINFUL REFINEMENT

*"But by God's grace I am what I am, and His grace
shown to me was not wasted. Instead, I worked harder
than all the others—not I, of course, but God's grace
that was with me." – 1 Corinthians 15:10, International
Standard Version*

My undergraduate experience literally became a
fight for my life and maybe even my soul. I was forced
to learn to stand spiritually in order to remain
spiritually, mentally and emotionally strong.

During my numerous conversations with my

mother, she provided scriptures to encourage me. However, as a young man, I wanted immediate help lifting the heavy burden, not a scripture, so I would exclaim, "There ain't no God who would let me go through this!" Yes, I was extremely angry at God because my ability to navigate this part of my journey was totally out of my control. All of the tools I had acquired to help me get to this point in life were no longer useful. This part of my life was in God's hands.

As an immature follower of Christ, I didn't understand that it was necessary for me to go through this refining process. Although I was precious in the eyes of God, He had to remove my impurities so that I would come forth as pure gold. Some of my impurities consisted of pride, self-centeredness and total self-reliance. God used my mother, a woman void of formal education but a possessor of a doctorate in life to help purify me. My mother had proven worthy by God to keep me grounded and sane during these years.

One of my first personal experiences with God occurred while I was a sophomore. I needed to go home for some reason; during my drive, the spirit of God spoke to me about visiting our pastor from my church in DeFuniak Springs: Reverend Moore of Mt. Nebo Baptist Church. As I drove along Interstate 10, the Spirit of God descended upon me, and I was moved to the point of crying, a cry from the depths of my soul. Years later, I still do not have the proper words to accurately describe that experience because it was something beyond emotion. I recall being peaceful and feeling like my soul was rising up outside of my body. I remember talking with God and saying, "Yes, Father. I will go."

I had never been to Reverend Moore's home and didn't have the technology that we use today to navigate my way to his house. Instead, I had something much greater, the original engineer and architect – Jehovah Jirah, or the God who always provides. Once I agreed to go, the spirit of God led me to Reverend Moore's home without any trouble.

Through this experience, I realized for the first time that I could know God for myself, on an individual basis. It wasn't about me remembering scriptures my mother had given me, but about me recognizing the voice of God speaking to me and responding.

Reverend Moore was a good man with a gentle spirit. I thought a lot of this man, and my spirit was somehow connected with him. My mom had told me that he was diagnosed with terminal cancer and could no longer pastor the church; in fact, he was bed-ridden. I had an easy, casual conversation with Reverend Moore and prayed with him. Before leaving, I took my right thumb and lightly touched his forehead and drew the cross of God on his forehead.

Finally, I left Reverend Moore's home for my parent's home. I arrived home and proceeded to do things as normal. It wasn't until Reverend Moore died a few weeks later that I shared my experience with God and at Reverend Moore's home with my mother and God-Mother. I had countless other experiences as a college student that proved these were my formative years as a man and Christian.

I became so broken and went to such a low point after being academically suspended from school twice that I turned to God often. My pride and ego were shattered. In fact, these written words are the first time I have shared this academic humiliation with my family. I had always been the golden child, so facing suspension and other issues that I didn't want to share with my family forced me to look to God for support, guidance and hope. On several instances, I took my transcripts, laid them on the floor with my books and all my other course materials, fasted and prayed, literally falling asleep on the scattered materials.

Through the scriptures my mother had given me and divine destiny, I kept getting back up, standing and fighting my way through the struggles. I was learning to stand on my own, without succumbing to the temptation to quit or calling my mother for reassurance. The scriptures that my mother had been giving me all my life were like seeds that finally found good ground in my heart and started to grow within me. I began to develop a blind faith in God and to believe His Word. I resolved that I would endure and stand, whatever I faced and whatever the cost. Sure enough, the trials kept flowing my way.

One night after completing mid-term exams, my girlfriend and I walked into my apartment. As I made my way to the bedroom, I noticed a shadow of someone who seemed to be looking in my window. Without thinking, I punched the glass out of the window and seriously injured my right wrist, cutting nerves, tendons and my left elbow. If the cut had been a few centimeters deeper, I would not have been able to use my left arm.

While my girlfriend and best-friend drove me to the hospital, I passed out because I had lost so much blood. When I awoke, surgery had been performed, my parents were standing over me with my girlfriend and best friend. Even in the midst of this unfortunate situation, I recognized God's goodness.

My surgeon, who I consider to be one of God's angels, did not charge me for the surgery. Based on the invoice, the surgery cost more than $17,000. In addition, the hospital bill of more than $5,000 was waived as well. Why and/or how do I explain the fact that I wasn't charged for these medical procedures? For me, the simple answer is Unmerited Favor. God was demonstrating His great love for me and the fact that He would always take care of me. Through these experiences, I was gaining an understanding of God's grace on my life that granted me things I did not earn.

Since I could not use my dominant writing hand, I had to take the semester off. This setback caused me to experience some level of depression. I am no psychologist; however, as I reflect and having later worked with individuals with mental health issues, I am certain I dealt with depression during that period of my life.

But God is faithful. I bounced back, reenrolled in school and completed my undergraduate studies.

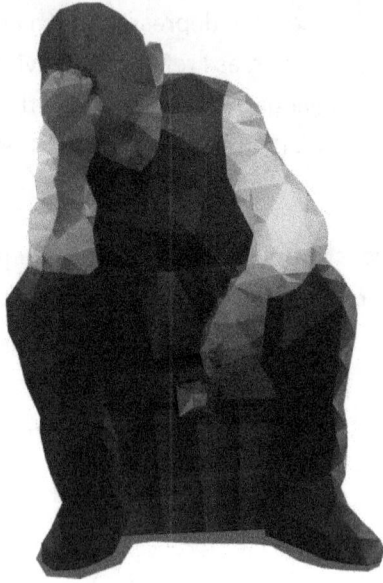

CHAPTER 6: THE LAND OF EGYPT: PUTTING ON NEW SKIN

"This ordinariness doesn't become you" -T.D. Jakes

Before graduating college, I depended on my parents to help sustain me financially. Finances were not my primary concern; finishing college was my focus. Though I struggled with getting books and course supplies on time, most of what I had to stand against during those years had nothing to do with money but more with maturation.

My college experience afforded me the

opportunity to shed my pride, self-centeredness, self-reliance and childhood tendency to quit whenever I felt like it or didn't like what I was facing. Encountering the new world of responsibility, problem solving and stress associated with earning a college degree facilitated my emotional, mental and spiritual development into a man. I encountered obstacles, setbacks, and the consequences of bad decisions, but I persevered. However, I was as a college graduate filled with anger.

I had worked tirelessly to earn a degree in a field that I had no desire to work in; therefore, I didn't pursue any engineer-related employment opportunities. In fact, I didn't even care about the degree because I felt pursuing Engineering was about my mother, not me. Therefore, I gave my Bachelor's Degree in Engineering Technology to my mother. I had earned the degree because of her influence, but I stood against starting a career in Engineering. I knew my strengths were not in that field and felt I had suffered enough for something I didn't want to do.

My first job as a college graduate was in higher education. Florida Southern College (FSC) in Lakeland, FL, hired me as an admissions counselor with a salary of $17,000 a year before taxes. In terms of financial status, the job was definitely a demotion from my middle class upbringing. Though my daughter Ashley stayed with me in Tallahassee every summer while I was in college, I didn't have the full financial responsibility of a parent year-round while in college. Child support accrued during my college years, but I didn't have to pay it while a student. Upon graduation, I had to pay more than $10,000 of child support in arrears on a $17,000 a year salary.

To make matters worse, I was informed by then college President Dr. Thomas Reuschling that I was not the first candidate chosen for the position. The first candidate selected a different opportunity, so I was offered the position. Starting this incredible journey was a complete culture shock for me because I had just spent six years at the largest Historically Black College or University in the country; now I found myself at Florida Southern College as the first black professional in the institution's 110 year history as the second choice.

Here I was a college graduate with a degree that I never planned to use, making a salary that did not require a college education, working in a completely foreign environment as a second choice and needing to pay accumulated child support while still being available for my daughter. Yes, I was angry and knew this could not be my situation for long. The desire to rise above my position had nothing to do with a bad experience at FSC. In fact, my experience with Dr. Reuschling as my mentor gave me the very professional foundation I stand on today.

In conversations with my parents about my career, they always pressed upon me the career model with which they were familiar, which was working 30 years or more with the same employer then retiring. I listened to them and others and wanted to comply, yet everything within me pushed me to go a little further and dig a little deeper.

I knew at my core that I would never fit into the box my parents and others were comfortable with and seemingly needed in order to exist. To me, they were asking me to settle with being ordinary, but my internal mirror's critique of this costume I was being implored to wear was altogether different. In its quiet, still voice, my conscious said, "This ordinariness doesn't become you."

Though I wasn't earning much money and my path to obtaining my position didn't do much for my ego, I obtained valuable work experience and thoroughly enjoyed my job. I was extremely passionate about my role as an Admissions Counselor because I recognized parental influence as a major factor for determining a child's success on any level but especially in the post-secondary process.

Plus, my experiences gave me firsthand knowledge of the troubles the wrong parental guidance could create. Since my mother did not have the background to help me in this choice, she influenced me down a path that could have been detrimental to my self-esteem, ambition, destiny and life. I didn't want anyone suffering through the issues I had endured as an undergraduate student. Therefore, I seriously counseled students and parents about parental influence, college prep courses and college acclimation.

I developed immensely as a professional at FSC. My passion and work ethic led to the opportunity for me to develop a multi-cultural affairs office, which cultivated keen administration capabilities, community relationship leadership and program development skills within me. I worked extremely hard with the campus community and external community to make FSC more accessible and pluralistic in its social and cultural offerings for students.

I worked so diligently to develop the office and was so passionate about equipping others to avoid the pitfalls I encountered that I was selected as a Carl Brown Fellow by the National Association of College Admissions Counselors (NACAC). Part of the distinction included spending a summer at Claremont McKenna College (CMC), *a highly selective, independent undergraduate liberal arts college 35 miles from Los Angeles,* to research and present my work. During my summer at CMC, peers from around the country came to participate in the professional seminar offered by NACAC. More than 100 people attended my presentation.

While I developed as a professional at FSC, my spiritual growth continued. I actually began my CMC presentation with the biblical story of Jacob wrestling with God and man. Though my supervisor at the time advised against it, stating that it wasn't a relevant connection, I felt compelled to share the story, so I obeyed what I felt I was being called to do by God. In a fairly dramatic way, I connected the story of Jacob wrestling with God to my personal experience in establishing the FSC multi-cultural affairs office.

By Kobra Bunkley

Broken, But Blessed...

And a man wrestled with him until the breaking of the day. When the man saw that he did not prevail against Jacob, he touched his hip socket, and Jacob's hip was put out of joint as he wrestled with him. Then he said, "Let me go, for the day has broken." But Jacob said, "I will not let you go unless you bless me." And he said to him, "What is your name?" And he said, "Jacob." Then he said, "Your name shall no longer be called Jacob, but Israel, for you have striven with God and with men, and have prevailed." Gen 32:22-32

LESSON:

Brokenness is the path to blessing. Before God can use a person greatly, He must break him or her because we all have a built-in propensity to trust in ourselves.

People who have ever wrestled know how exhausting it is to grapple with an opponent of equal or greater strength. A few minutes of such activity is enough, but Jacob kept at it all night. The meaning I take from this account is God showing Jacob the power of his self-will. The Lord kept waiting to see if Jacob would surrender his will to God's will, yet Jacob kept fighting.

I relate to Jacob greatly from childhood through this time in my life and professional career. More specifically, I wrestled with God throughout my undergraduate experience. If I had to endure the six year wrestling match with only my child-like mindset, I never would have made it. But God spoke through my mother the essential tool I would need to endure this fight for my life, which was to stand.

When God taught me to stand properly, it was more than just the literal meaning of the word. He taught me to stand for His will, not my will. God put His very heart and character in me to stand for what I believe is right, to stand against the trials in life, to stand on His Word that heaven and earth would cease to exist before one word of His scripture would fail and finally to stand and believe that God has a divine purpose for my life.

Overall, the evaluation of my CMC presentation was outstanding, and the content I shared about building and fostering a multi-cultural affairs office was very well received. However, I received mixed feedback about my biblical metaphor. A few of my peers didn't think the story about Jacob wrestling with God was necessary. On the other hand, I saw one of the senior advisors crying as I shared the account of Jacob. I may never know who that message was for, but if God received the glory, that is all that matters to me.

The critical character traits given fertile ground to grow in me at FSC were a strong work ethic, a passion for higher education, oratorical skills, a commitment to helping others and the desire to achieve. One of the many opportunities for me to exhibit my professional growth was serving as keynote speaker at the Martin Luther King Jr. celebration on campus. In fact, I was the key-note speaker for three years consecutively. As I researched and prepared to deliver the speeches, I learned more about Dr. King's legacy as well as his most prominent speeches and writings.

This time of profound learning and growth were dampened by the realization that the same issues which existed in society then prevail today. The same kind of people who perpetuated social issues in the past use the same tactics presently. Once I began to understand certain realities (the existence of a glass ceiling, the fact that I would have to compromise personal truths to get ahead, my ability to get ahead was controlled by someone else and my capacity to provide for my family could be limited by someone else), I came to acknowledge that I was in a modern day Egypt.

Like the children of Israel, I was in bondage, only professionally. As long as I stayed in the land of Egypt, I would remain a slave and have to submit to the harsh realities noted above. This epiphany probably happened for me so early because of my daughter Ashley. As a father desiring to provide a certain quality of life for my child, I was highly motivated to establish a financial legacy founded on spirituality, hard-work and a good name so that she could stand on my shoulders and go a little further in her academic pursuits and professional aspirations.

Furthermore, I knew God's plan included me enjoying a vibrant life, in perfect harmony with the gifts He had given me. So, I refused to allow my life to be a series of random events, orchestrated by others' perception of what was right and/or good. Therefore, I determined to live life on purpose and with passion at a rather young age.

LESSON:

True happiness for me is knowing I am constantly in the process of becoming what God meant for me to be, and the Lord wants no less for you! From my life, I share the following Bible lesson and truth: **Do Not conform any longer to the ways of this world, but be ye transformed by the renewing of your minds (Romans 12:2).**

In the eyes of others….

Gary was hired at a time when I wanted to change the culture of FSC to be far more hospitable towards minorities. In Lakeland, minorities had a negative perception of FSC. To many, FSC was a school for rich, white kids. Gary reached out to the local African American community in Lakeland. It was important to have the community understand that FSC was making a meaningful effort to recruit and retain minority students. The effort took diplomacy and social skills. Gary helped persuade our local minority constituency that FSC would be a nurturing place for their children.

However, Gary instinctively knew that minority enrollment would only stabilize at a meaningful percentage if recruited students felt comfortable and valued on the campus, so he worked hard to help establish organizations and activities on the campus that supported our minority population. Gary made FSC a better place through his youthful exuberance, organizational skills and rapport with students. He had a knack for making good things happen.

-Dr. Thomas Reuschling, President Emeritus, Florida Southern College

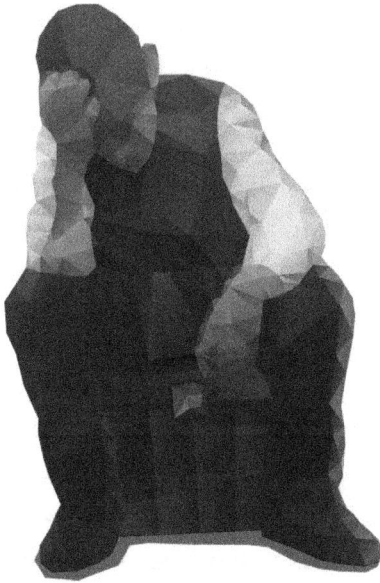

CHAPTER 7: LIVING LIFE ON PURPOSE

"In order to reach your next level of greatness, you must keep going, you must keep growing, you must maximize your potential and you must expand your capacity" -Gary T. Hartfield

After more than two years at FSC, I knew it was time for me to ascend to the next level professionally. I felt a Master's Degree in Business Administration (MBA) would afford me more options to pursue a career in higher education. Yet, I made this decision with great heartache.

From a logical perspective, I chose the MBA program for several reasons. I knew I was limited professionally with my specific, technically oriented undergraduate degree. An MBA would provide a broad range of career options. Based on my research, it seemed prestigious and laudable to have earned an MBA. I figured having an MBA on my resume with an undergraduate degree in Engineering Technology would present me as accomplished and intelligent to human resource professionals looking for bright, new talent. Finally, the MBA was the best degree option available to accomplish my ultimate goal at that time, which was to earn a Ph.D. in Business Administration and continue on the Higher Education Executive career path.

While at FSC, I set the goal to navigate my way to the presidency of a four year university. My ultimate goal was to become President of my alma mater, Florida Agricultural and Mechanical University (FAMU). My plan was clear, but I was still torn.

Emotionally and spiritually, I had literally poured myself into building the multi-cultural admissions and affairs programs at FSC, so I was reluctant to leave the seeds that I had planted. Then, there were the people, including mentors, friend and students, who had impacted my life that I would need to leave.

While contemplating this change, I drove around Lake Hollingsworth in Lakeland listening to Lionel Richie & the Commodores' song "Jesus is Love" with my heart full of sorrow. The lyrics of the song that resonated with me at that time are:

I wanna follow your star
Wherever it leads me
And I don't mind, Lord
I hope you don't mind

I wanna walk with you
And talk with you
And do all the things you want me to do
'Cause I know that Jesus

(Jesus is Love, I know) 'Cause I know, Lord
(And if you ask, I'll show)
(Love is the word forever) And ever and ever

After finally accepting the transition, I focused more on the next phase of my journey, graduate school. On pure faith, I left Lakeland and returned home for graduate school though I had not been accepted into the Master of Business Administration (MBA) program at the University of West Florida (UWF). In addition to my below average undergraduate GPA of 2.3, I made the minimum score required on the standardized admissions test. However, I was determined to seek God's promise of a better life. Sure enough, God opened the door. After a little more than a week of being home, I received conditional admission into the MBA program at UWF.

At this point, I began to fully live my life on purpose and with direction. I was focused and eager to demonstrate my academic ability in the MBA program. My dedication paid off, literally. I finished the first semester of the program with a 3.75 GPA and was awarded scholarship funding. During my first meeting with College of Business Graduate Advisor Dr. Timothy O'Keefe, we connected. I believe Dr. O'Keefe saw my earnest desire to achieve in the MBA program and as a professional; he immediately took a personal interest in my success.

As I matriculated through graduate school, I researched the profession at the professor and executive levels to assess if this career path would indeed be a good fit for me. One of the ideas within higher education that I had particular difficulty with was tenure. Since academic tenure is primarily intended to guarantee the right to academic freedom, it protects faculty members and researchers when they dissent from prevailing opinion, openly disagree with authorities or spend time on unfashionable topics.

I viewed tenure as a mask to hide the true intentions of a misguided professor. Giving an individual guaranteed employment with the exceptions of moral turpitude, financial exigency or incompetence seemed like the perfect structure for abuse of the system. The idea of promoting "academic freedom" is noble, yet, throughout time, humanity has done more harm than good within this type of construct.

Nonetheless, I saw obvious benefits of the notion of academic freedom, especially after reading Professor Robert Jensen's "What white privilege sounds like," Cornel West's "Race Matters" and many of the wonderful works by Nikki Giovani and Maya Angelou. I am grateful these intellectuals had the "academic freedom" to share their thoughts.

At the same time, it occurred to me that the men and women who have had a timeless effect on learning and humanity had no regard for "safety" or a "system" of protection. Instead, they seemed to live beyond a desire to be a part of a system that in one way or another would ultimately control them. Jesus, Martin Luther, Nelson Mandela and Dr. Martin Luther King Jr. are men who stood against the system; their words illustrate that they acted in defiance to the systems in place during their lives.

Jesus Christ: "I am the way, the truth, and the life. No one can come to the Father except through Me."

Martin Luther 95 thesis: "I cannot and will not recant anything, for to go against conscience is neither right nor safe. Here I stand, I can do no other, so help me God. Amen."

Nelson Mandela: "Difficulties break some men but make others. No axe is sharp enough to cut the soul of a sinner who keeps on trying, one armed with the hope that he will rise even in the end" -Nelson Mandela from a letter to Winnie Mandela, written on Robben Island, 1 February 1975

Nelson Mandela: "There is no easy walk to freedom anywhere and many of us will have to pass through the valley of the shadow of death again and again before we reach the mountain tops of our desires."

Dr. Martin Luther King Jr: "The ultimate measure of a man is not where he stands in moments of comfort and convenience, but where he stands at times of challenge and controversy."

In my opinion, these great men not only stood in opposition to the system but railed against it. They knew conforming would directly oppose their spiritual freedom; therefore, submitting to the system equated to death to them.

I took a few entrepreneurship classes during my MBA program, and in one of my numerous beneficial experiences in those classes, I worked on a consulting project. A classmate and I conducted a financial and management analysis and assisted with developing an employee manual for a local small business. The project exposed me to resources available through the Small

Business Development Center (SBDC) and allowed me to explore consulting as a career option. I began to see multiple avenues for a future career.

During my final semester in the MBA program, I was hired as Coordinator for Academic Support Programs at FAMU's College of Engineering Sciences, Technology and Agriculture. I started my position in May 1999, three months before graduating with my MBA. Needless to say, I was extremely proud that my decision to leave FSC and return to school had proved worthwhile because it truly was faith that caused me to take that step. As a result, I had earned a great job before graduating and seemed to be on track to fulfilling my goal of becoming president of my alma mater.

In the eyes of others....

Gary's personal attention during my admissions process sealed the deal for me to attend Florida Southern College! I had offers from Bethune-Cookman University and Abilene Christian University in Texas. I don't know what the outcome would have been had I chosen another college, so I'm always thankful for Gary in making this choice easy for me.

Gary is solely responsible for my introduction to Kappa Alpha Psi and decision to become a member of this fraternity. Being the first in my family to go to college, I really had no knowledge of fraternities or any type of Greek life. As a member of Kappa, Gary was very instrumental in bringing the interest of Kappa Alpha Psi on the campus of FSC. We made history and established the first historically black fraternity on FSC's campus. None of that would have happened had it not been for Gary originally sparking the interest!

As a professional, I really learned from Gary to put my heart in what I do. Gary was very passionate when it came to recruiting and maintaining relationships with students of FSC. He was not the type of recruiter who would recruit you only to never be heard from again.

The biggest lesson I learned from Gary is to make my career impact someone in a positive way because it's not always about the salary or status. Currently, I'm an Area Administrator with Orange County Public Schools

Food Services department. In my position, I oversee 27 schools and their cafeteria operations. I'm heavily involved in my church including mentoring, ushering, and singing in the men's choir. I'm married with a 12 year old daughter and 2 year old son.

Many students, including myself, considered Gary a big brother type who helped shape our path in our college journey! Gary will always be an important part of my life. Gary was a great role model for me to follow, and I picked up a lot of knowledge from him just in casual conversation. Anytime I think of Gary, a smile comes on my face. We had such good times and great memories! I'm blessed to have had him in my life!

-Tony Jenkins, Orlando, FL

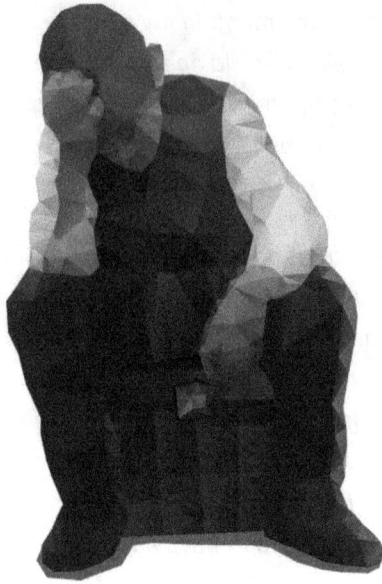

CHAPTER 8: DO NOT ENTER INTO THIS LIGHTLY

"(Marriage) is not by any to be entered into unadvisedly or lightly; but reverently, discreetly, advisedly, soberly, and in the fear of God." – 1789 U.S. Book of Common Prayer: The Form of Solemenization of Matrimony

When I transitioned from DeFuniak Springs to Tallahassee to begin my new position, my daughter Ashley came with me. Ashley's mother and I had a lengthy conversation prior to me moving during which she decided to allow Ashley to live with me. I thought her agreement was very significant and honorable. Ashley's mother loved Ashley with all of her heart, but she did not possess the tools necessary to help our daughter as a student. Her mother knew that I could give Ashley the academic support, experiences and exposure to help her become a successful student and young lady.

I wanted Ashley with me because I had witnessed her self-esteem and academic confidence diminish. She had failed Kindergarten and did not have solid academic support. I knew if Ashley completely lost her self-confidence then she would not have the opportunity to blossom into the woman that God destined her to be. Giving credit to my mother's teaching and guidance, I also knew it was time to help my daughter. Ashley's future was very fragile; as her father, I needed to step-up, so I did.

When Ashley and I moved to Tallahassee, we moved in with my fiancé. The arrangement was convenient for both of us. I had dated my fiancé for a couple of years on and off. She, too, had been a teenage parent and was raising her daughter as a single parent. I knew part of my job responsibility was to recruit for the College, which meant I would need to travel overnight frequently. Therefore, having Ashley in a stable environment where she could receive the proper support and encouragement seemed like the right thing for me to do.

After a few weeks of completing my MBA, moving to Tallahassee and starting my new job, I married my fiancée. I did not marry based solely on love and the prospect of building a future together. Part of the reason I married was for convenience since I had custody of my daughter, Ashley, during her formative years of school and maturation. We became a couple with two daughters: Ashley and my new wife's daughter.

On the surface, our life together seemed great. My new wife recently had completed her MBA. We both were Christians and committed to a local church, so we shared much in common. Unbeknownst to me, I would face new obstacles in the marriage and need to stand yet again.

I was extremely focused at this time in my life. I had a strong relationship with God, was doing a good deal of reading for enlightenment and stayed current with community affairs. The Pastor of the church we attended asked me to be the Church Administrator. At the time, I was not sure what the responsibility entailed, but I agreed because I had a good relationship with the Pastor.

When the Pastor asked me about compensation for fulfilling this role at the church, I quickly replied, "No, sir. No form of compensation is required." My response was based on my observations and readings related to ministry, work and money. With the honor of being the church administrator and my wife being appointed over youth education, we seemed to be moving in the right direction.

However, this time proved to be pivotal for our marriage. As the church administrator, I was approached by several people with rumors that the Pastor was having an extra-marital affair with at least one of the young ladies in the congregation and possibly more. On several occasions, I asked my wife not to bring this issue to me because I did not want the distraction in our home. After asking her to respect my wishes repeatedly, she finally blurted out while in the car driving home one Sunday after church service the rumors she had heard regarding the pastor.

With this outburst and by disrespecting my request, my wife failed to realize that our marriage was irrevocably broken. I was adamant about not bringing the nonsense into our home, but my wife disrespected a very simple request. Although on the surface this one mistake by my wife seemed like something we could overcome, it was not. We did not have a solid foundation to build from and help us endure the trial and test of time. We did not have love. Our relationship and marriage were never the same and slowly declined into a miserable, sad state.

To worsen the situation, I asked my wife, after she had disregarded my wishes about discussing the messy rumors, about leaving and finding another church home for our family. I did not want to be involved in the foolishness and didn't want us or our daughters exposed to it. My wife's response was not only surprising but disappointing. She exclaimed that I was a quitter, and we needed to stay to endure this test instead of running from the issue. I learned that my wife had numerous casual conversations with my mother. As a matter of course, my mother informed her how I frequently quit football as a child. My mother shared these stories with my wife in jest. It seemed, based on her comment to me about quitting, my wife thought I was still the old Gary.

After some time, I resigned the church administrator position and grappled with staying in the marriage. Staying in the marriage for the sake of convenience and the children was not the right thing to do. The summer of 2000, after the first 10 months of marriage, I wrote my wife a letter explaining that I was leaving. The letter detailed my belief that being married to her was not the right place for me because I was not planted in good ground and would never be the man God called me to be as long as I was with her. I left the letter in a conspicuous place for her to find when she came home from work.

I made alternative living arrangements for Ashley and me; however, after a short separation, I returned. We endured in the marriage for five more years. My wife and I had several separations, going back and forth, and I experienced countless sleepless nights. After our initial separation, my second daughter was conceived. The pregnancy was difficult for me because I grappled with the strength of our marriage.

My second daughter Imani was born September 7, 2001, four days before the 9/11 attacks. From the day Imani was born, we have had a special relationship. She is the first child I helped to raise as an adult and with the means to fully provide for her. As her father, I accepted my responsibility to love, protect and provide for her no matter the circumstances.

The final separation occurred between my wife and I the summer before Ashley's senior year of high school; the divorce was finalized in November of 2005. The fall-out that the arguing, separations and divorce had on Ashley and Imani cannot be measured. Though Ashley had been equipped with the necessary tools to successfully finish high school, I know it was difficult for her to move back to DeFuniak Springs and be separated from me, her step-sister, her baby sister and friends. I know Ashley has emotional scars from the marriage, separation and subsequent divorce.

When I married, I was very immature and entered the marriage based on convenience. I did not consider the love, patience and sacrifice that would be required from me to help our marriage grow. After nearly a year of dealing with frustration and set-backs in the marriage, I committed adultery. I did have remorse, but my heart was so distant from my wife that I did not care about the consequences the act would have on my family. I felt more ashamed and grieved that I had disappointed God. I tried to be a good provider and father in the marriage. However, I failed miserably at being a good husband.

For years, I carried animosity against my ex-wife. Ironically, I did not fully forgive her until July 23, 2014, as I was writing this chapter of the book. My ex-wife texted me and asked me to forgive her for her part in destroying our marriage. I took a few hours to respond, but I knew it was God. Who else would have caused the message to be sent while I was writing this chapter?

I finally responded to my ex-wife that I forgave her and asked her to forgive me for my part in destroying our marriage. After nearly 10 years, the circle became complete, and my ex-wife and I could both heal fully. I believe however tumultuous my journey, it will always be worth it if I learn something from it.

From the roller coaster of marriage, repeated separation and divorce, I learned there is a heavy price to pay for entering into marriage lightly. I paid figuratively and literally for marrying for convenience; however, the price I had to pay was well worth it because God will never have to teach me those lessons again.

I also discovered several aspects about me. I clearly know characteristics I want in a significant other; I learned to keep my words and the dynamics of my relationship to myself. Finally, I learned that I must demand respect from my significant other because if a woman cannot support me with respect, the relationship will never work because respect is my love language. I can be in a relationship with someone for years and if she never utters the words, "I love you," I may never notice. However, if my significant other respects me, it is one of the greatest expressions of love for which I could ask.

So much for entering into marriage lightly. The lesson comes full circle for me when I acknowledge that my primary reason for marrying was to help save my daughter Ashley. In the end, the way I did it was not a good choice because it ultimately cost me a big part of my relationship with my daughter. Other alternatives to marriage were available at the time. I simply didn't know how to access them. In spite of the pain and hurt that the separation cost my family, I knew I had to take a stand by leaving. If I didn't leave, I would have allowed the situation to spiral out of control and consume me, my future and ultimately, the future of my children.

"Is not marriage an open question, when it is alleged, from the beginning of the world, that such as are in the institution wish to get out, and such as are out wish to get in?"

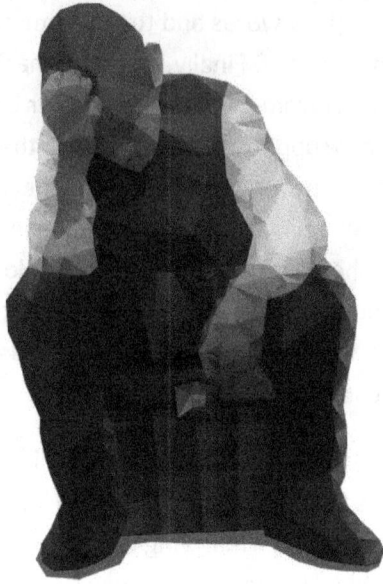

CHAPTER 9: ORDINARINESS NEVER SUITED ME

"Philosophers have long conceded, however, that every man has two educators: 'that which is given to him, and the other that which he gives himself.' Of the two kinds the latter is by far the more desirable. Indeed all that is most worthy in man he must work out and conquer for himself. It is that which constitutes our real and best nourishment. What we are merely taught seldom nourishes the mind like that which we teach ourselves." — Carter G. Woodson, The Mis-Education of the Negro

I was extremely proud of the opportunity to go back to my alma mater and serve as a professional after earning my MBA. I enjoyed some great successes as Coordinator of Academic Support Programs at FAMU's College of Engineering Sciences, Technology and Agriculture (CESTA), but I eventually became disheartened about building a career in higher education.

During my tenure at FAMU, I am humbled to acknowledge that we developed some successful programs. We formally adopted Miami's Coral Reef Senior High and William H. Turner Technical Arts High School to serve as feeder schools for our Engineering and Agricultural degree programs. We also established an experiential learning opportunity with Gainesville Regional Utilities (GRU) for our Electronic Engineering Technology (EET) students.

Additionally, I helped to establish an experiential learning opportunity with Sprint for one of our professors to work at the Sprint headquarters in Kansas City, MO, in order to gain exposure to the latest in communications technology. The professor was tasked with bringing real-world experience to our students. Furthermore, I custom built a database utilizing Microsoft's Access to assist me in recruiting and enrolling students for our academic programs. After facilitating the adoptions of the two secondary schools in Miami and being awarded the "Hardest Worker Award" at the University, I was promoted to Director of

Academic Support Programs by the FAMU President.

My experience at FAMU afforded me various opportunities to further explore whether I wanted to pursue a Ph.D. and my goal of becoming a college president. I interviewed the University President and Provost to inquire about their experiences and to seek guidance. Both men were delighted that I asked for interviews and seemed interested in my growth as a professional in higher education administration.

Given my experience at Florida Southern College (FSC), I had a certain expectation when I signed with FAMU. The only point of work reference I had at the time was my experience at FSC, where the President and my immediate supervisor invested financially and otherwise in my efforts because they realized the return on their investment.

As a professional and a FAMU alumni, I was happy to build bridges to help more students experience studying at the historical institution. I utilized all of the skills and competencies acquired at FSC to help me be successful as a professional at FAMU.

However, after careful consideration and observation, I decided not to pursue the goal of becoming a university president. I became disenchanted with the idea and solidified my position on the ineffectiveness of tenure in higher education. After two years at FAMU, I knew my time was drawing to an end because this "ordinariness" was not becoming to me. I began to feel the box was far too small. I wrestled with the idea of resigning; in the back of my mind, I heard my parents' admonishment: "You need to get somewhere and stay there."

In my career search, my strategy of leveraging my technical undergraduate degree with the MBA seemed to be rather effective. During a career fair I attended, I had the pleasure of meeting a recruiter for a company that was the world leader in the investment casting of super alloys, aluminum and titanium primarily for jet aircraft engines and airframes as well as industrial gas turbine (IGT) engine components. After a great introduction and engaging phone interview, I was actively recruited to work in Virginia Beach as a Sales Engineer.

During the career fair, I also was reconnected with a professional friend who had worked at a local university doing similar work in Multicultural Affairs at the same time I was with Florida Southern College. The young lady had resigned from Stetson and was working in Orlando, Florida, for the largest benefits outsourcing firm in the world at that time. She convinced me to submit my resume with the firm.

Though my heart was set on the career opportunity with the engineering firm, their hiring process was taking an extremely long time. I waited approximately four months before making my decision.

Since I was growing weary of my tenure at FAMU, I decided to take the job in Orlando at the benefits outsourcing firm.

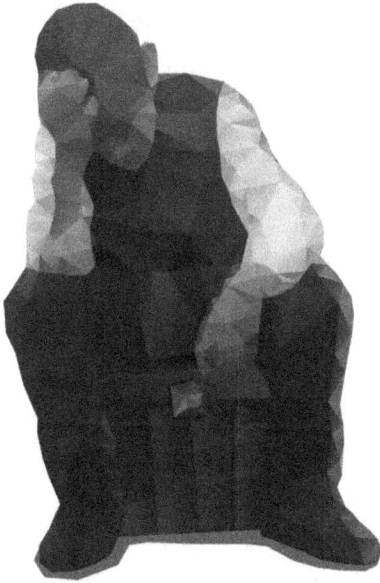

CHAPTER 10: THE WILDERNESS

"I freed a thousand slaves. I could have freed thousands more if they knew they were slaves" –Harriet Tubman

Accepting the opportunity at the benefits outsourcing firm worked well for me financially because I received a relocation and signing bonus. I used part of my signing bonus to invest in my first investment home. The home, which was located next to my parents in DeFuniak Springs, FL, was in foreclosure. I purchased the home for approximately $22,000; however, it was worth more than $60,000 at the time.

Within a few months of purchasing, cleaning and renovating the home, my dad rented it out. The house has stayed rented since I purchased it in 2001, proving a valuable investment. In fact, only two renters have been in the home since I purchased it; the first renter lived in it until her death in 2012. The second lessee has lived in it within two months of the first renter's death.

Though I made an excellent financial move by leaving FAMU, I knew almost immediately that I would not "fit in" at my new job; it was my first experience in corporate America. The company's culture was to work 10-12 hours a day, which meant even if I finished my work in 8 hours, I needed to remain at work. The unwritten rule dictated that I spend another 2-4 hours at work for face-time, if nothing else. I perceived the company as a cold and sterile work place.

In spite not feeling like an integral part of the culture, I was able to demonstrate a level of success in my assignments. The assignment I am most proud of was leading the quality assurance testing of the interactive voice response (IVR) system for a large new client. Quality assurance testing includes developing and implementing a test plan to make sure the system being tested responds correctly to all given input. The programmer and I developed and tested the system with such effectiveness that we were asked to develop a template to be used for best practice within the company.

Very soon after I started work, the HR Recruiter who hired me, resigned her position. When I asked why she was leaving so soon after recruiting me to the company, she responded that she didn't fit in and found herself in a position where she felt like she constantly had to defend and protect herself against some peers in HR.

Company decision makers decided to take the company public in 2002. An integral part of the initiative included promoting diversity within management ranks. To help groom diverse managers and acclimate associates to the company's culture, the organization developed affinity groups for Black employees, Latin employees and the Diversity Council.

Additionally, any employee identified as a potential manager was assigned a mentor. I vividly remember my mentor. From our initial conversation, I knew this individual was a company man with no personal interest in my growth outside of the benefits he might receive if I did well because then, my success would reflect well upon him. I equated my mentor's energy to the energy I felt from some of the self-serving coaches I had growing up when I played sports.

As President of the black affinity group in Orlando and a member of the organization wide Diversity Council, I had an opportunity to be a part of conversations and meetings to which my peers were not privy. Ultimately, I was positioned to stand for who I was, who I represented and what I believed.

During one of our Diversity Council meetings that included Senior Management for the site and the Diversity Council leader from our home office, the Center Leader for HR stated, "I feel minorities think they are entitled to management positions." The context in which she made the statement was being asked to give her opinion on the lack of diversity in Plan Management and management within the center. After making this statement, she quickly realized she was in the "mixed" company of blacks and whites; the other senior managers were embarrassed by her comments. The Diversity Council leader quickly changed the subject, suggesting that we return to the topic. So, we did what was convenient for my white counterparts and placed the issue in the "parking lot."

I was completely surprised by the statement that the Center Leader for HR had made and was even more disgusted and frustrated with the dynamics of the organizational experience. After this meeting, I understood, in no uncertain terms, why the HR Recruiter left, why no minorities were in management, why the culture was so foreign and why I did not fit in.

I clearly understood how the Center Leader for all HR matters, including recruiting, retention and succession planning, was led by someone with prejudicial sentiments toward minorities and no sensitivity or diversity training. The running joke among the "minorities" was that we worked for the largest benefits outsourcing firm in the world and were supposed to be subject matter experts in all things HR – including diversity. However, when anyone took a look at the profile of the staff and management employed at the organization, diverse would not be an adjective used to describe us.

I interviewed a manager for a personal project I was doing to help me navigate the cultural roadway at the organization. As Delivery Group Manager, this man was responsible for hundreds of associates' recruitment, retention and succession planning. The gentleman was white and openly gay. By this time, I had had numerous conversations with the gentleman and found him to be direct and to the point, which I appreciated.

During my personal interview with him, the gentleman became really comfortable talking to me. When I asked how many minorities he was doing succession planning with, he replied that he thought all Latinos were lazy. After making the comment, he realized that he had a made an insensitive statement and apologized. Regretfully, I didn't directly address the statement he made by seeking clarification. Instead, I disregarded the comment and continued the interview. During the remainder of the interview and until this day, I often have wondered if he had this to say about Latinos, what did he have to say about African Americans and other minority groups?

My experience at this organization was my professional "Tipping Point." It was the magical, majestic and mystical moment I realized that "this ordinariness does not become me" and I had the right to live my life and choose my path. I decided not to try to conform to the box, realizing I was bigger than the box, so it would never be enough to contain me, no matter how hard I attempted to conform. For all intents and purposes, it was my "wilderness," or my land of just enough.

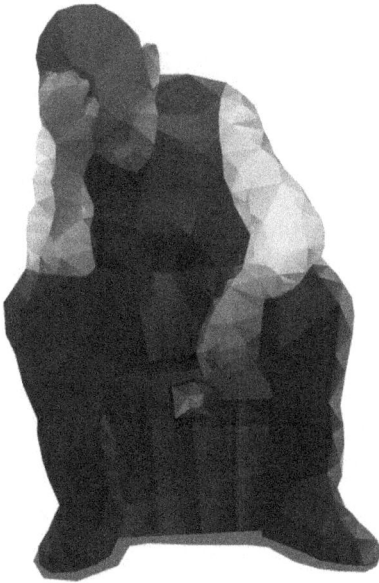

CHAPTER 11: MY OYSTER EXPERIENCE

"The essential thing is to find the vision, the passion, the purpose that you are willing to stand for – your personal truth. A truth that rings true for you and when trouble comes and you have no other course – you STAND for this truth!" –Gary T. Hartfield

While employed at the benefits outsourcing firm, I started looking for entrepreneurial opportunities that would help me create financial independence and realize my potential in the land of more than enough.

While visiting my sister Tammy in St. Petersburg,

FL, one weekend, she suggested that we look into owning an Assisted Living Facility (ALF). My sister Tammy possessed a deep passion for working with the elderly and developmentally disabled, which originated while she worked with the local Agency for Retarded Citizens (ARC) in our hometown. While living in St. Petersburg, Tammy was exposed to various Assisted Living Facilities where she lived. Tammy and I discussed the idea a few times, but I had concerns about my sister's overall ability to maintain sobriety on the road to recovery from her long battle with a crack cocaine addiction. After speaking with my sister at length and visiting facilities in St. Petersburg, I began the journey to financial success.

My prayer was and remains to be able to provide for my family and myself without the fear of not being myself and holding fast to my personal truths. I am so thankful to serve a living God who heard and responded to my sincere, honest prayer. Utilizing the skills I acquired while earning my MBA at the Small Business Development Center, I contacted the local office in Sanford, FL, where my family and I were living at the time.

The advisor I worked with was very helpful and thoughtful as I began to navigate this course. He carefully explained that I would need to know my business better than anyone who worked for me in order to maintain long-term success.

Our initial plan was to purchase land in our hometown and build a 30-bed assisted living facility. With this in mind, I began writing the business plan. I wrote and researched, researched and wrote until nearly 3:00 in the morning. I felt as if I was suffocating at the place where I was employed, so I was literally "writing for my life." I woke up every week day, after writing until 3:00 am and arrived at the job by 9:00 am.

While at the firm, I started to develop agonizing stress aches in the back of my neck. It would be so painful that I couldn't sleep comfortably at night some times. I was so uncomfortable in this situation that everything within me, as a man, kicked into survival mode.

I describe my experience at this company as my oyster experience. Most precious jewels are found buried in the earth; however, pearls are found inside a living creature: an oyster. Pearls are the result of a biological process, which is the oyster's way of protecting itself from foreign substances. When this happens in nature, an oyster develops a pearl. In my case, the foreign substance was the foreign culture at the firm that I could not and was unwilling to acclimate to. I became so uncomfortable that I developed the willingness to step out on our entrepreneurial idea, and I developed a pearl in the form of a business vision.

While writing the business plan, I visited my hometown to visit established ALFs in the area to network, conduct field research and inquire about operations. One individual to whom I will always owe a debt of gratitude is Francis Howell, who owned Howell ALF. This amazing woman answered all of my questions and provided practical information about how to run an ALF. With Mrs. Francis's help, I bridged the theoretical research on establishing and maintaining an ALF with the actual daily nuisances that cannot be captured on paper.

After nearly a year and a half, the business plan was ready. I had completed a 30 page plan that included a 3-year pro forma, marketing plan and architectural rendering of the proposed facility on the proposed site. During this time, I travelled between Sanford and DeFuniak Springs, six hours one-way, to complete the zoning process for the proposed site. I made this trip several times during the process. Each trip, I didn't know what to expect from the City Council. However, I knew I wanted something better than what my position at that time offered.

Getting financing was another step that my sister and I had to take simultaneously with the zoning process. I approached 1st National Bank in Destin, FL, with the project. After a few months of going back and forth with my Loan Officer, we were offered the possibility of securing a Small Business Association (SBA) loan. The loan required an 80/20 injection, which meant the SBA would finance 80% of the project if I could inject 20% into the project. Given that the total estimated price of the project was $500,000, we needed at least $100,000.

I had more than $30,000 in equity from the investment property I had purchased back home, but I was at least $70,000 short. I tried every possible avenue that I could conjure to raise the money, but nothing materialized. After exhausting every possible means of financing, Tammy and I gave up on the project. I had done all I could do, so the only thing left for me to do was stand.

But God...after not being able to execute the initial plan, my sister came up with the brilliant idea of buying a smaller existing facility in the St. Petersburg area. After some research, we visited a small, eight bed facility in Seminole, FL, which is located near St. Petersburg. After negotiating with the owner, Tammy and I finalized the deal. The purchase agreement was $170,000 for the home and $30,000 for the business, a total of $200,000.

After closing, my sister and I went to Macaroni Grill for a celebration lunch. We returned to her apartment in St. Petersburg where I napped and Tammy went to work as a waitress at a local restaurant. When I awoke, I returned to Sanford to pick up my daughter Ashley.

Around 7:00 am the next morning, I was awakened by a disturbing phone call from my father explaining that the paramedics could not get my sister Tammy to breathe. I couldn't wrap my mind around what he was saying; given Tammy's past experiences, I thought she was sick or hurt but would be fine.

My father called back several minutes later and said, "She's dead, Gary"…just like that, my sister was gone! Approximately 14 hours after we closed on the business, my baby sister was dead. I fell to my knees and exclaimed, "My baby's dead." This was the first time that my daughter Ashley had seen me cry. I had not given her the bad news that Tammy had died from respiratory arrest; she had taken an over dose of OxyContin.

I went to St. Anthony's Hospital in St. Petersburg to see my sister. As I walked in to see Tammy, the pain and grief went away. Tammy was beautiful and angelic on the examining table. Although she had a perm, her hair returned to a natural curly texture and her face seemed to glow. My baby sister looked as if she had finally found peace. Tammy struggled with her addiction to crack cocaine and OxyContin. My sister's prayer was if she could not control her addiction and take back her life that God would take her home to find peace.

Before Tammy's death, we shared a few biblical terms and scriptures as we navigated the business venture process. We repeatedly discussed the terms patience, faith and wisdom. When I left the hospital after her death, I noticed that Tammy had written those three words on her calendar inside her bedroom.

During Tammy's funeral services, I spoke about what patience, faith and wisdom meant to us. By God's grace, mercy and the revelation of the meaning of these terms through the study of them scripturally, I have received the abundant blessings God intended for me to have.

Patience: Let Patience have her perfect work so that you will be perfect and entire; lacking nothing. (James 1:4)

Wisdom: Wisdom is the principal thing therefore get wisdom. However in all thy getting, get an understanding. (Proverbs 4:7)

Faith: Faith is the substance of things hoped for and the evidence of things not seen. (Hebrews 11:1)

I believe Tammy, who is one of my guardian angels, left me two gifts to let me know that although I could no longer see her, she was never far away; the first gift is a picture of a little girl smelling an orchid with a quote below it about IMAGANITION. The quote states, "You cannot begin to IMAGINE what God has in store for you." The second gift is a key chain in the shape of an angel with Exodus 23:20 on which; the scripture reads, "Behold, I send an Angel before thee, to keep thee in thy way, and to bring thee into the place which I have prepared."

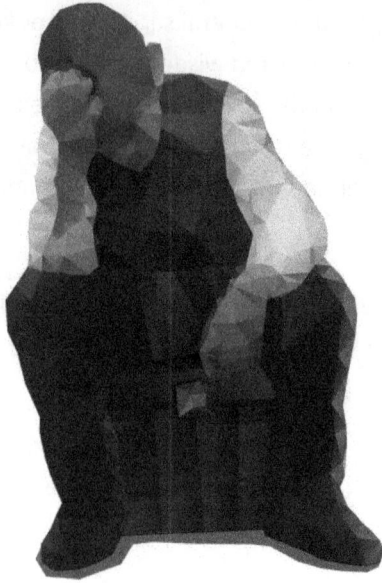

CHAPTER 12: MEETING THE REAL ME

"It is an absolute human certainty that no one can know his own beauty or perceive a sense of his own worth until it has been reflected back to him in the mirror of another loving, caring human being" –author unknown

As I became more and more financially independent, personal parts of my life would be challenged. Growing up, I often was reminded by my sister that I didn't resemble her or my older brother Booketee Jr. The amazing aspect of youth and innocence is that while I heard my sister, it never dawned on me that I was somehow "different."

Most of my parental bonding occurred during my childhood years with my mother; I was very close to her. Normally, I didn't think twice about leaving my mother to play with other kids in the neighborhood. However, at certain times, I longed to be near my mom for no known reason. I didn't need to be close to her; I just needed to know she was there. One of the things my mother and I did together was grocery shop; it was one of our special times together. I pushed the cart, ran over her heels and probably frustrated her a lot, yet this was our time.

During my primary years, my father did not live in Florida. Though he and my mother were married, my father lived in Illinois because the job market was better there, particularly for his skill-set. My father was a machinist; he used various tools and machines to make airplane parts for his employer, a government defense contractor.

Though my dad lived in Illinois, he travelled home on every occasion he could. I remember the excitement my siblings and I had whenever daddy came home. It was an exciting time, and he usually brought gifts.

When I was about 10 years old, my dad moved home to stay. Though I don't recall the dynamics of the move, I vividly remember the impact. I had grown up under my mom's guidance and instruction; however, things changed drastically when my dad came home. Almost immediately, grocery shopping with my mom and other things we shared together came to a screeching halt.

My dad felt I shouldn't be doing those things; instead, he thought I should be working with him mowing yards, which was his side job. Although I didn't mind mowing yards, I did not like the fact that my dad came and changed the dynamics of the house and my relationship with my mother.

I resented my father for the change and other things. For one, he lacked the ability to communicate with me. He yelled at me and made me feel that I needed to defend myself against him; my father's yelling was constant and almost overwhelming. Also, my father disciplined me like he had something against me. Most of the time I ran or tried to find ways to defend myself. I didn't feel my father disciplined me out of love; I felt he was beating me to try and break me.

As I grew older and stronger, so did my resentment towards my father. I repeatedly told myself that he couldn't be my father and treat me like he did. One day, with tears in my eyes, I told my mother there was no way that he was my father treating me like he did. My mom was standing in the kitchen putting canned goods in the cabinets. When I made the statement, she turned and made a peculiar face. I was about 12 years old at the time and still remember the look on my mother's face: it was a look of surprise and curiosity, as if someone had told me one of the deep, dark family secrets that no one knew.

As time elapsed, my formative years were filled with this love/hate relationship with my father. As I grew older, stronger and taller, I was able to defend myself against the physical altercations, but the emotional battle remained. I became shell shocked over the years from the constant yelling. As a man today, I resent when people yell at me. I respond by shutting down and becoming very defensive.

When I left home for college, my father told me that I would never make it. I don't recall the content of the conversation, but like most things that I endured with him, I tucked his remarks away and did not deal with them until writing this book.

My father and I stopped communicating after we had a very explosive argument when I returned home after earning my bachelor's degree. During that time, I was rebuilding my self-esteem and needed a familiar place to recuperate. Almost immediately, the yelling started when I returned home. The difference was, as a college educated young man, I yelled back. I became very defensive, and deep down, I wanted to fight my father. I wanted to get him back for all of the things I felt like he had done to me.

One day, I moved some of my father's clothes

without asking his permission to make room for my clothes. I moved some of his clothes out of the closet in my room to a different closet and placed the clothes that I assumed he didn't wear in the garbage outside of the house. My father was livid when he noticed. He went on a yelling and cursing rant that really bothered me. I found myself cursing and yelling back at him with the boldness of a man. I exclaimed I don't need him and would pack my things and leave, so I did. I was about 24 years old at the time.

I was 26 years old before my father and I began to establish a relationship again. I was working in Lakeland at Florida Southern College at the time. One day while leaving work, the burden was lifted, so I started to reach out to my father. I thank God for resiliency and forgiveness.

I learned that my father grew up during very tough circumstances. Originally from McClain, Mississippi, he was kicked out of the house by his step-father and left to survive on his own at age 14. I imagine being on his own at 14 and trying to maintain himself was very tough. My father probably endured some of the worst cruelties mankind has to offer. To this day, my father does not know who his biological father is. Based on my father's facial features, hair texture and skin tone, we presume his father was either white or of Latin descent.

After my sister Tammy's unexpected death, my oldest brother Rodney and I were sitting in her apartment having a casual conversation about Tammy and other members of our immediate and extended family. Suddenly, Rodney mentioned that the man I thought was my father was not my biological father. I asked whether it was an assumption or fact. He responded that it was factual, that my older sister Kim and I share the same biological father.

Although surprised by this news, I already knew that "Pa was not Pa" in my heart of hearts. Based on the way my father had treated me, as opposed to his biological kids (my brother Booketee Jr and sister Tammy), I knew he couldn't be my father.

I was 33 years old when I learned this news. I contacted my mother, but she didn't confirm or deny the fact. Her refusal to deny the fact was confirmation for me. I began to reach out to my aunts and uncles about this information; one of my aunts confirmed everything and gave me a complete account of events.

Subsequently, my mother reluctantly confirmed the identity of my biological father. I guess she needed to protect my biological's father marriage as well as her own. I contacted my biological father, and we met for lunch and talked. The first thing my biological father said to me was, "I apologize. If I were you, I would hate me." After he apologized, all of my negative thoughts and reservations left. My spirit was totally free to develop a relationship and receive him as my biological father.

For the first time in my life, I could see myself in my father. I was 34 years old and could finally self-actualize; I could perceive a sense of my worth because I could physically see it reflected back to me in the mirror of another loving, caring human being. Ironically, I looked more like my father than any of his other children.

For young men, identifying and actualizing with their father or some other positive role model is important to maturation and leading a productive lifestyle. Understanding this, good fathers are intentional about modeling good behavior in front of their sons. This phenomena is also done with mentoring. In various mentoring programs, young boys are paired with another positive role model in the community. The same practice is demonstrated in the professional arena because it is pivotal for young men to interact with, watch and emulate another loving, caring human being, specifically another male. This form of modeling helps to provide young men with self-confidence, self-worth and a foundation from which to stand as they set out to become men and carve out their own path.

Once connected, my father and I had a wonderful time talking; he knew most of what had occurred in my life. Behind the scenes, he had always been present with financial support. My father attended both of my undergraduate and graduate school graduation ceremonies. Of course, he didn't sit with my family, but he was there. My father's apology gave me peace with him and the situation. I could not feel anger or resentment; after he apologized, I felt relieved and open to develop a relationship with him.

On the other hand, my mother did not apologize and offered every excuse imaginable concerning why she never revealed my biological father. Because of my mother's unwillingness to admit her wrong, I began to resent her. All of the memories from me growing up with the man I thought was my dad equally became a part of her committed offenses. I felt she allowed me to suffer under the hands of this man who probably knew I was not his child, although the secret had never been told. The hatred and resentment I felt for the man who disciplined me so severely was rendered valid, and my mother was equally culpable.

I developed a wall against my mother, and her credibility became zero to none with me. One day, I had a heated conversation with her and explained that the difference between my biological father and her was that he simply apologized. I explained that she used every excuse she could conjure up and never stopped long enough to admit her wrongdoing in the matter and simply apologize.

My mother eventually apologized. Today, I am redeveloping my relationship with her. My mother is such a positive part of all that I am and hope to be. We talk daily on the telephone. I call to check on her health status and get the daily update on the local community and family members. Our relationship will take some time to fully redevelop because I still carry a sense of betrayal and pain from this experience. However, my mother will always be the rock I lean on for spiritual guidance and comfort.

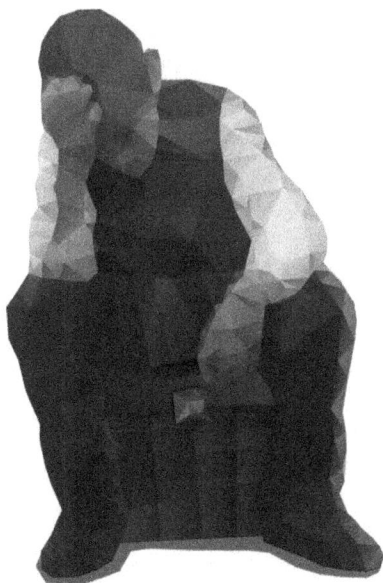

CHAPTER 13: REVEALING WOUNDS

*"A week later his disciples were in the house again,
and Thomas was with them. Though the doors were
locked, Jesus came and stood among them and
said, 'Peace be with you!' Then he said to Thomas, 'Put
your finger here; see my hands. Reach out your hand
and put it into my side. Stop doubting and believe.'
Thomas said to Him, 'my Lord and my God.'" –John
20:26-28*

This chapter describes an important lesson I
learned from an extremely challenging professional
chapter in my life; it is a lesson I am continually

reminded of and will most likely continue to apply in life. The lesson is that, like Christ, as we "reveal our wounds" with others, people can find comfort or confirmation in God's Word that helps them to endure moments of disbelief in order to stand through life's difficulties.

Polk County Opportunity Council, Inc., better known as PCOC, is a private, non-profit agency located in Bartow, FL, responsible for administering approximately $12 million in funds from Health and Human Services (HHS) for Headstart and Early Headstart as well as funds from Florida's Department of Community Affairs (DCA).

PCOC is a Community Action Agency (CAAs); CAAs are nonprofit private and public organizations established under the Economic Opportunity Act of 1964 to fight America's War on Poverty. These agencies help people to help themselves in achieving self-sufficiency. Today, approximately 1,000 Community Action Agencies serve the poor in every state as well as Puerto Rico and the Trust Territories.

I have always stood against injustice and enjoyed working with organizations committed to fighting injustice. I worked with PCOC as a consultant for a period of time before being hired as its Director of Operations. From the day I became an employee to the day I resigned, the agency was embattled.

After careful research and interviews with staff and the community, I learned the agency had a long history of people management issues in addition to a dysfunctional Board of Directors. Not every board member failed to perform his/her duty individually, nor did a general perception exist that the Board, as a whole, did not perform its duty. Nonetheless, I found myself under poor leadership. To further exasperate the internal issues and public perception problems, the Chairman of the Board refused to seat a member or representative from the Bartow City Council, a refusal that directly violated the by-laws of the agency.

I was informed that the Chairman refused to seat the individual from city council because he believed the person was racist and would ultimately attempt to shut down the agency by creating chaos and confusion. The chairman's perception of this individual was based on him having similar dealings with an agency that was defunded. I also was informed that city officials met privately with the board chairman and executive director to encourage them to seat the individual in order to avoid the scrutiny the issue created. Despite the reasoning of the officials and other individuals, the chairman refused. Assuming this defensive posture ignited a series of unfortunate incidents that could have been avoided.

The agency faced several external and internal issues at that time from HHS, the agency's funding agency. Shortly after being hired as Director of

Operations, I was tasked with helping with the public relations nightmare as well as with helping to oversee the fiscal office. The fiscal director had been fired and the senior accountant was being investigated for taking federal documents from the agency and sharing them with individuals outside of the agency. Removing these documents from the agency was a federal crime. Furthermore, the individuals and the office(s) involved in the meeting were culpable as well. I was informed by the board attorney that officials from HHS, the local congressman's office and others were at this meeting. The local newspaper had assigned a reporter to cover the issues at the agency.

I recommended that the Board pursue this matter given evidence that the documents were stolen and the Office of Management and Budget (OMB) Circulars establishes specific fines and penalties for stealing federal documents. The Board Attorney communicated with a representative from the congressman's office regarding this matter, but to my knowledge, it was never followed up on.

After approximately one year with the agency, the Executive Director resigned and I was promoted from Director of Operations to Interim Executive Director. Before the Executive Director resigned, I was approached by two members in senior management and a board member regarding seeking the Interim Executive Director position. The two senior managers arranged a meeting with the same Board Chairman who refused to seat the representative from the Bartow City Council. During this meeting, they recommended that the current Executive Director be asked to resign and I be named the Interim Executive Director.

I was asked by the Board member to provide a list of issues he could use as ammunition to encourage the other board members to ask for the Executive Director's resignation. I played into both of these plots just as well as the senior managers and board member. As a young, aspiring and slightly naive professional, I was mesmerized with the excitement of hearing my name.

In retrospect, this was one of the worst decisions I have ever made as a man and professional. Poetic justice occurred when the same people who betrayed my predecessor and set me up for the position betrayed me. In that case, I got what I deserved. It was a costly and painful lesson learned; however, I am a wiser professional and better man because of it.

During my first 90-days as Interim Executive Director, the financial arm of the Federal Bureau of Investigation (FBI) was in my office. Officially, they were from the Office of the Inspector General (OIG). In addition to managing the engagement by OIG, the agency had to complete and implement a plan of corrective action for the many issues listed in the Single Audit, the finding from HHS, the public records requests as well as manage a staff of more than 100 people with a $12 million budget.

It seemed that the Congressman's office, HHS and others' strategy to defund the agency was to inundate it with bad press and a constant barrage of audits by various state and federal agencies. I was informed by members of the Board and local community that the motivation for the attack on the agency was to award the local school district with the funds from HHS for Head start and Early Head start.

To make matters worse, the branch manager for the regional office of HHS terminated the agency's ability to draw-down funds to meet payroll and accounts payable liabilities. After several emails and phone calls, the attorney and I took a flight to HHS in Atlanta, GA, to address this concern. We flew to Atlanta the same day payroll was due. After meeting with superiors of the person who suspended our ability to meet payroll and advising them of the situation, we were given the ability to draw-down funds. I called the office immediately and had the senior accountant complete the payroll process before we left the HHS office.

The strategy I employed to help save the agency was to define the critical areas to focus my energy on then begin to systematically address them. The critical areas I defined were relationship management, operations management and people management.

Our efforts in relationship management included developing a relationship with all levels of staff at HHS,

DCA and progressive individuals and organizations in the community to solicit for guidance and potential board members, seeking local board appointments that would give me visibility and access to key influencers in the community and asking the Congressman to recommend a board appointee for an in-person meeting.

We were successful in all efforts except developing a relationship with the Congressman. He agreed to meet with the new board chairman and me. However, I felt his mind was made and everything was set in motion to defund the agency and give the funds to the local school district.

Most of the issues that HHS and the Single-audit cited as deficiencies were fiscal issues. To resolve these issues and build sustainable systems for fiscal management, I hired an independent contractor to help fix the issues. I also restructured the Fiscal Department staff; the restructuring included terminating and reassigning members of the fiscal team. Finally, we facilitated an open bid for a new agency to conduct our single audit.

The independent contractor, a Certified Public Accountant, led the agency through the following year's audit. We recovered from a "Disclaimer of Opinion" (lowest possible opinion) on our previous year's audit to a "Qualified" opinion (2nd highest opinion). In addition, I was informed by the board attorney that the agency received a letter from OIG that stated, in summary, though the agency had serious fiscal issues in the past, it seemed to be moving in the right direction with current leadership and there were no issues of fraud and/or theft.

We addressed each citation systematically and with the intent of restoring the credibility of our cognizant agencies as well as the public. We made significant progress during this time of constant duress. However, the board made a significant mistake just as the agency was beginning to recover.

After consulting with an attorney, I informed the board about the history of an organization they were considering hiring to do some work; the organization, Mid Iowa Community Action (MICA), did not possess a good history with the type of engagement the board envisioned for them, so I recommended that the board avoid it. However, due to perceived pressure by our cognizant agencies, the board entered into a $100,000 sole-source contract with MICA.

I was on vacation when the board allowed the MICA team to come into the agency to help put systems in place. The engagement with MICA was paid for by agency funds and grant funds that HHS and DCA allowed. I informed the board this contract directly violated OMB guidelines for procurement as well as Florida's guidelines. I found it interesting the same agencies citing the agency and threatening to defund it because of improper procurement practices allowed this action.

MICA's first order of business was to get rid of my independent CPA contractor, which the board allowed. MICA presented a general ledger to the board that positioned the payments to the CPA as a waste of money. MICA's specific duties were to help resolve any remaining deficiencies identified by the cognizant agencies. I purposefully detailed MICA's scope of work in the contract. The team-leader of MICA insistently tried to find ways to work beyond the scope of the contract. I found myself in a constant battle with the leader of the team. The team-leader was specifically interested in our back-up and work papers from our single audit.

During the engagement, someone on the MICA team leaked a report of their findings to the local newspaper. The board and others were outraged at this ugly attempt to discredit the agency. In the end, the MICA team retracted its comments and apologized. At least one of PCOC's board members wrote a letter to the MICA board explaining his disappointment and frustration with the ill-advised release of the report to the local media and how the engagement was handled. Shortly thereafter, the Executive Director of MICA was terminated.

The final critical area for me to address and correct was people management. During my experience at

PCOC, the most formidable, persistent issue was the work culture. A number of staff understood our mission and responsibility to the public and served the agency and community well. However, an even larger number of individuals embraced a mentality of entitlement and minimalism at the agency.

Entitlement manifested with an attitude among employees that they could show up for work (most of the time late) and think they were owed something simply for coming to work. The employee mindset was, "I don't have to give much, but I expect my employer to give me something — respect, pay, promotions, etc. — just because I show up."

Based on my research, the attitude of entitlement originated with some board members who influenced hiring decisions and/or promotions. The entitlement manifested in the employees in numerous ways, including resistance to feedback, an inclination to overestimate talents and accomplishments, a tendency to be demanding and overbearing, blaming others for mistakes and little sense of loyalty.

The problem was so integrated into the fabric of the agency that a human resource consultant advised me to restructure the entire agency. The restructuring meant every position would be open for employment, and the entire agency would be reorganized to best utilize all of its human, technological and financial resources. I presented the reorganization plan to the board for review. Needless to say, the board members who caused the problems were the first to offer a dissenting opinion. In order to truly move the agency in the right direction, we needed to restructure the board first and then the staff.

A number of reputable individuals supported this vision, yet the dilemma for me was how to sell the idea of getting my boss to fire himself! In a rationale and sane world, I could propose this idea as best for the agency. However, some members of the board had personal agendas that far-outweighed the needs of the agency.

Although the barrage of attacks prompted by the Congressman and other noted parties were significant, we were able to weather those storms. The storm the agency could not withstand was the storm from within, perpetuated by some members of the Board. Mark 3:25 is inherently true in this situation and for all entities and relationships; it states, "A house divided against itself cannot stand." In my estimation, the personal agendas of certain board members led to the defunding of the agency. We could have managed all the other issues, but the dysfunction of the board ultimately led to the demise of the agency.

After paying MICA $100,000 as requested by HHS and DCA, all of the deficiencies were supposed to be corrected and the agency was ready to move forward. HHS scheduled a follow-up visit with a team of reviewers; the reviewers were external consultants and the regional HHS Branch Manager came along to accompany the team.

I advised the board of the visit and prepared the agency for this review. As part of the review, I asked my IT person to set-up a video camera in the conference room where the reviewers would be working. I had done this exact same thing the previous time HHS had visited the office. My impetus for having the video camera was to protect the agency's documents. As I mentioned above, I had been informed earlier that members of HHS were present when federal documents were stolen from the agency and shared with them and someone from the Congressman's office.

The day of the review went as expected until the reviewers noticed the IT manager changing the tapes in the video recorder. I took full responsibility for not informing the reviewers as a professional courtesy that the video camera was in the room. What I did not know was the video camera was also recording audio. In Florida, it is illegal to audio tape someone without consent. I admitted to the incident, taking full responsibility.

I had the option to stand against the occurrence or tender my resignation. In light of the turmoil, not being certain whether the full board would support me and the Congressman telling local media that he wanted the State Attorney's office to investigate the matter, I chose to resign.

The experience at PCOC helped me to realize that a person's greatest strengths can also be that person's greatest weaknesses. My greatest strengths are an unrelenting desire to stand against injustice and a fervent desire to get the job done. These two strengths proved my greatest weaknesses at PCOC because I did not complete the most critical step in problem solving, which is to clearly define the problem.

An old Chinese proverb states, "for every one hundred people hacking away at the leaves of a diseased tree, will there be one who will stop and inspect the roots?" In the situation at PCOC, this meant, "Did the board, responsible for the governance of the agency, demonstrate the capacity (will and ability) to fully support me during this tumultuous time for the agency or when everything was brought back into compliance?"

I failed to ask critical questions about the board, my relationship to the board and how much I should invest in fixing the problem before seeing progress. Instead, I became so consumed with fighting what I perceived to be an injustice and working to get the agency on the right course that I never stopped to analyze the roots.

Due to my fervent desire to get the job done coupled with my firm stance against injustice, I allowed myself to become so personally invested in the issues that I began to make the unfair treatment about me rather than the agency. I spent a tremendous amount of time and energy, working 10 to 12 hour days, to correct the issues, placing my heart and soul in what I did to the point that I didn't separate myself from the agency. Though I take pride in my work ethic and "do whatever it takes" mentality to complete a task, this experience revealed the downside of taking that attitude to the extreme.

I received phone calls and emails from a number of people in the community wishing me well. Their consolation was thoughtful and needed; however, I truly would have liked to have finished the job. Throughout my time at PCOC, I often exclaimed to my mentor and others that I could handle the job to get the agency back on the right track, but I could not handle the politics. I guess I spoke my end into existence.

A few weeks after giving my resignation, I was arrested at my home. It's funny that the arresting officers did not know the charge; it was so obscure and meaningless the officers had never encountered it before. My arresting officers were polite and decent. I pleaded no contest to the charge and adjudication was withheld. As my lawyer spoke in court, I looked at the prosecuting attorney and judge to see if they had a soul. I don't remember neither of them making eye contact with me.

The pain, anger and disappointment from this experience and how it ended were immense. It took me several years to come to terms with my time at PCOC and ask God to forgive me for being prideful and taking everything so personally. I also asked God for the strength to forgive all of my counterparts. God helped me to realize that forgiveness was not simply about my colleagues, but it was more important for me so that I could heal and move on with my life.

Looking back, I regret allowing selfish pride to lead me into making this professional mis-step with my counterparts, especially since I knew their intentions. I regret not being present personally to receive the letter from OIG and the other agencies which stated we had brought the agency into full compliance. Most of all, I regret that I was not able to finish the job and help save the agency.

Nevertheless, I count this experience all joy because I developed in some significant areas. I am certain that I will make more mistakes as I continue on life's journey, but I will never make this one again.

LESSON:

James 1:2-4,12: "Consider it all joy, my brethren, when you encounter various trials, knowing that the testing of your faith produces endurance. And let endurance have its perfect result, that you may be perfect and complete, lacking in nothing. . . . Blessed is the man who perseveres under trial; for once he has been approved, he will receive the crown of life, which the Lord has promised to those who love Him."

Trials and tribulations will come; they bring the following purposes and rewards:

- To bring discipline or new life/light
- To raise you to the next level of faith
- To bring you into your purpose

CHAPTER 14: ENTERING THE PROMISELAND

"In order to reach your next level of greatness, you must keep going, you must keep growing, you must maximize your potential and you must expand your capacity." -Gary T. Hartfield

Serenity Village, the business that my sister Tammy and I started right before her death in 2002 served as a foundation for future businesses. In 2004, I invested into a lease-purchase agreement to acquire the second facility, Serenity Village II, Inc. In lieu of purchasing the second facility out-right, I used the lease-purchase option to better position me as the buyer and demonstrate my financial capacity to repay the debt to the bank.

The terms of the lease purchase agreement were 36 months with a $2,500 monthly payment and $5,000 down payment. At the end of the term, I purchased the facility for $300,000. I had $50,000 in lease-purchase equity in the facility; therefore, the final purchase price was $250,000; I had to pay all closing costs.

To close on the deal, I needed $10,000, which I borrowed from my parents. One of the things I am proud to say about my dealings with my parents and whomever I do business with or who does a favor for me is I try to be a man of my word. My parents were excited to be in a position to help me in this endeavor and gave me the money within a few days. I felt like a better man as I was able to repay my parents and give them extra.

The original facility and the newly acquired one were licensed as Assisted Living Facilities (ALFs) with a Limited Nursing specialty license. My business plan was to invest into a new facility every two years and continue to expand the business.

In 2007, I was introduced to three gentlemen who would forever change my life; they are Austin "Bud" Llewlyn, John Snell and Frank Gemma. These men had invested with another individual to provide Group

Home services for the developmentally disabled.

Unfortunately, the relationship did not work, so they were left in a precarious position of either trying to sell the investment home and business or identify another partner to manage the group home. We met and discussed the terms of the partnership; we have partnered together ever since. After a few months of settling in with the new business, we started to turn a profit with the business and everyone was pleased with the outcomes.

Given our success with the first investment partnership, I invited these three gentlemen to invest into shares of the existing facilities that I owned, Serenity Village and Serenity Village II. We came to terms on each of the facilities and agreed to equal partnership in each one.

I continued to expand the businesses. In 2008, I started Serenity Village - Adult Day Training (ADT) center for the developmentally disabled. Simultaneously, I started Serenity Village – Center for Self-Sufficiency, Inc, a non-profit 501 (c) (3). In February 2013, I invested in Serenity Village IV group home, purchasing this facility as sole owner from an embattled non-profit provider.

In 2011, I invested in a Liberty Tax franchise with my business partner. My partner and I were extremely successful in our first year of business. However, we noticed we still had all of our fixed costs to manage without the luxury of having revenue to meet the expenses during the non-peak months for tax preparation. To help resolve this issue, we opened Serenity Insurance and Sweettalk Wireless in December 2012 as a means to generate revenue year-around in our tax offices.

While I planned some of the businesses, others were divine destiny. However, I can attest that all of the businesses have been protected and sustained by God's favor. Though God's favor has been on each business, everything has not been easy or flowed smoothly. On the contrary, there have been some very tough times. At times, my chest began to ache because of the stress and worry; I doubted God at times; I broke down and cried at times; I had to fast and pray for a break-through at times; through it all, God provided me with a way to overcome my obstacles through my mother and father.

When I was at the point that I felt like I couldn't bear my responsibility any longer, I called my mother, who reminded me and refreshed me with these words, "Don't you know that God didn't bring you this far to leave you?" With those powerful words, I was given the strength to not only persevere but continue to move forward. Often, I was reminded of the old Negro spiritual that stated, "I think I'll run on to see what the ends gone be; run on to the end, to see what Jesus has for me." Like my mother, my father was always in the background with anything I needed. It was comforting to know he was a phone call away, no matter the circumstances.

Through God's favor and Tammy's dream of owning an Assisted Living Facility, we have been blessed to grow and expand our initial investment of $200,000 into a multi-million dollar enterprise. A key to our success is based on my guiding principle and God's law recorded in Matthew 7:12, "Whatsoever in all things you would that me would do unto you, do you also unto them. For this is the law and the prophets."

What I saw lacking most in the working world was the willingness of people to pour into others, the desire to make a meaningful investment in someone beyond self. Therefore, I deliberately decided to share with my managers and other interested parties pearls of wisdom as a means of investing and depositing into them what God has given me to educate, empower and motivate others to pursue their purpose. Later, I learned and realized what I am doing is being a good steward. I am giving my time, talent and treasure unselfishly, just as Jesus did for those around Him.

God's promise for good stewardship is simple: to "bring ye all the tithes into the storehouse, that there may be meat in mine house, and prove me now herewith, said the Lord of hosts, if I will not open you the windows of heaven, and pour you out a blessing, that there shall not be room enough to receive it" (Malachi 3:10).

The simple truth is that of all the forms of making money, if you tithe, all of these things will be added to you so that you will not have room enough to receive it. Although this very simple truth is real and tangible, very few individuals truly realize this potential return on Investment (ROI) because of a lack of faith.

LESSON:

When I STAND before God at the end of my life, I would hope that I wouldn't have a single bit of talent left and could say – I used everything that you gave me – Erma Bombeck

In the eyes of others...

Gary's Christian faith helped draw us together; we share spiritual values. I initially met with Gary before introducing him to the other two business partners. Gary and I spent several hours talking. I felt comfortable right away. Once we met with the other two guys, we moved forward. With all of his talents and strong personality, there is a humility in Gary that rounds him out; he's a total person.

-Bud Llewelyn, business partner

Gary brings an incredible entrepreneurial ability that I rarely see in other people to the table. He can look at a business from a lot of different angles. He truly has a gift when it comes to business. One of the things that Gary does well is really empower the people underneath him. The four partners meet regularly to review business. There are 30+ folks who work for us; Gary can speak to all of them from a professional level. The employees are spread over 3-4 different towns over a 24 hour shift, yet Gary takes an interest in them, teaching them the business, how to do the paperwork and keep things in order.

-Frank Gemma, business partner

It if wasn't for Gary, there wouldn't be a Serenity because we were about to lose it due to a bad partnership. Gary is a compassionate yet very bright businessman; he possesses a unique set of tools: compassion, business intelligence, teacher and mentor. I think Gary finds, hires and trains the right people, which are three distinct skills. As a sales manager, I know that finding versus hiring versus training the right people is difficult. I count Gary as a friend as well as a business partner and am impressed with His caring, compassionate side.

-John Snell, business partner

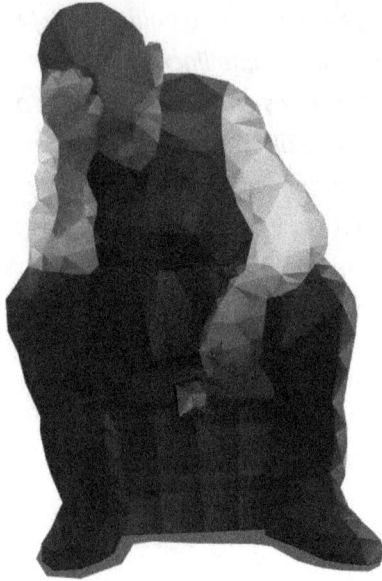

CHAPTER 15: ENTREPRENEURIAL
FAITH: A SPIRITUAL BATTLE

"No spirit so effectively robs the man of his passion, purpose and potential, as the spirit of fear" –Gary T. Hartfield

I realize that as someone called according to God's purpose, as a Christian and as a man with a God given vision who is earnestly pursuing that vision, I have entered into a spiritual battle.

Throughout my life, the job of my enemy, the devil, has been to utterly destroy the promise, potential and purpose in my life before a testimony could manifest that could be used to help others and uplift Jesus Christ. God's Word states in John 10:10, "that the thief cometh not but to steal, kill and destroy."

The first verb is **"cometh."** Note that scripture does not say "might cometh" or that the thief may not visit you. The devil is walking to and fro in the earth trying to find whom he can devour; therefore, it is inevitable that you will be tried by him. The question is not will Satan visit but when will he visit!

The second verb is **"steal,"** derived from the Greek word kleptos. In modern English, we use the derivation kleptomanic to define an individual who cannot resist the urge to rob or steal from someone. The devil desires to steal vision, potential, passion and purpose before they begin to grow. If the spirit of fear can rob you at an early stage, it has a greater chance of keeping the vision from coming to fruition and a greater chance of utterly destroying your life.

The third verb is **"kill,"** derived from the Greek word thuo. In the context of this scripture, kill does not mean to physically murder the individual. It is translated more appropriately to "give up." Through the spirit of fear, the devil's plan is to steal passion, purpose and potential and kill the fruit that you would bear by forcing you into a position of surrender, to give up. Satan wants you to give up on your relationship, marriage, vision, business, career, faith…to give up period.

The final verb is **"destroy"** from the Greek word apollumi. In the context of this scripture, destroy means to put "out of the way" entirely, abolish, put an end to, render useless. Satan ultimately desires to put an end to passion, purpose and potential and render you useless.

However, that same scripture ends with Jesus declaring, "I am come that they might have life, and that they might have it more abundantly" (John 10:10). Once I realized that Jesus already paid the price for me to enjoy my life, I was determined to receive everything He had died to give me.

I had to STAND on the promise of God to give me not only life, but an abundant life. I had to choose to stand up against the thief so that he would not leave me broken and cynical in my mind, with my family, in my career, in my emotions or with my finances.

Satan wanted to perpetuate the spirit of fear into every aspect of my personal, educational, financial, professional and spiritual life. The thief attempted to create fear through people, conditions and situations in such a horrible way that I could not see a way to solve problems except to give up everything that remained, leaving me hopeless and defeated. I realized the enemy's ultimate aim was to devastate me.

I wrestled with the spirit of fear in the early stages of investing in the business. The spirit of fear kept me awake with nightmares. The spirit attacked me when my sister passed away after we purchased the business. I lived two hours from the business and worked in corporate America. The constant fear was I could not maintain my job and manage the business. Fear created pain in my chest caused by stress and anxiety about maintaining the business. I struggled with meeting payroll, paying the mortgage and making financial ends meet. I almost didn't obtain licensing, which would have caused us to lose the business due to poor management.

The same spirit of fear that tried to keep me from stepping out on faith to start a new business tried to prevent me from falling in love, pursuing an advanced degree and ultimately, from surrendering my life to God. Though Satan attempted to steal, kill and destroy in my life, God's grace and mercy caused me to persevere through the initial attacks.

The next round of attacks came through the people closest to me, family members who somehow felt entitled to the success of the business. I faced jealousy from immediate and extended family members. The conversations I had with my mother about this topic caused me to get so incensed with her that it forced me to reach out to God and further establish a personal relationship with Him.

I endured these attacks by STANDING on God's Word. I had to communicate my resolve to family members that I had no intention of giving them anything or any part of the business. They were not there when I struggled to keep things going, so I did not feel it was fair for them to want to jump on the bandwagon after things seemed to be going well.

Even at this stage, nearly 15 years after starting the business and expanding it to its current status, I still must STAND against the spirit of fear. Satan still tries to attack utilizing many of the same tactics that he used before. I realize that he enters the mind to try to get me to react to this roaring lion. However, Satan cannot do anything without me responding to him.

In my life's experience, the spirit of fear has tried to take on many forms, but its intentions remain clear: to keep me from fulfilling the destiny that God has on my life and stop me from living a joyful, spirit led existence where I give to others out of the overflow of love in my life. To combat and defeat the spirit of fear, I use the scripture, "For God gave us not a spirit of fear but of Power and Love and Self-Control" (2 Timothy 1:7).

- The spirit of Power, derived from the Greek word Exousiazo. In modern day English, this means to exercise authority over, to have authority. In this scripture, God gave us power over the spirit of fear. God gave us the authority to command this spirit to depart and never return.

- The spirit of Love, derived from the Greek word Agape. Agape love is most notably defined as "unconditional." Because God is the very definition of Love, Love is the most powerful force in heaven and on earth. Thus, God's love is the antithesis of fear.
- The spirit of Self-Control; the Greek translation of Self-Control is "the bringing of men to a sound mind." The evil forces of this world have no arms, no legs and no means to utter words. Instead the spirit of fear enters the mind and controls a person's arms, legs, mouth and ultimately, mind. The battle against the evil forces starts and ends with a person's ability to control self. More specifically, people must control what they allow to enter into their mind. The weapons given to us to help control self is the spirit of power and the spirit of love.

LESSON:

There is an inextricable relationship between the spirits of Power, Love and Self-Control. However, the battle starts and ends with a person's ability to control self. The spirits of power and love must be used to establish and maintain self-control. Maturity in your relationship with God will give you the wisdom to use these weapons more decisively. The spirit of fear has no power unless you give it. If you can control self, you can control the spirit of fear.

SACRAMENT

"In view of your sharing in the gospel from the first day until now. I am confident of this very thing, that He who began a good work in you and will perfect it until the day of Christ Jesus." Philippians 1:5-6

You may ask, "Why is it necessary to offer a sacrament in a memoir?" My response is the same as it was when I presented the story of Jacob during my fellowship presentation: I was compelled to do it.

For the purpose of this chapter, sacrament is defined as an outward sign of an inward grace. The sacrament I offer is this memoir of my life as I stood against attacks, developing as a man, Christian and business owner, in the process of moving from the land of not enough to just enough to more than enough. From my story, my hope is for you to receive education, motivation and empowerment.

Ralph Waldo Emerson once stated that the mind once stretched by a new idea will never return to its original dimensions. I hope that my sharing has sparked new thoughts, created new ideas and permanently changed the dimensions of your mind. I hope your perspective of what is possible has been forever changed and you will never settle for "Not Enough" or "Just Enough" again. I hope that you will never allow ordinariness to become you and you always strive to live in the land of "More than Enough."

Finally, I hope that you will continue to expand your mind, broaden your horizons and walk into your destiny.

EPILOGUE: IN THE FULLNESS OF TIME

"If you really want to understand what it takes to be successful, don't ask, 'What does it take to get to the place that you are at?' But rather ask, 'Who and what did you have to give up?' Success is inextricably related to sacrifice" –Gary T. Hartfield

In Physics, I learned about Sir Isaac Newton's Three Laws of Motion. Although I can draw a parallel between all three of the Laws of Motion to success and sacrifice, I will use only the third law to not bore the reader.

Newton's third law states that for every action, there is an equal reaction equal in force but opposite in direction. Simply stated, this means that when an object pushes another object, it gets pushed back in the opposite direction equally as hard.

To illustrate this concept, consider the flying motion of birds. A bird flies by use of its wings. The wings of a bird push air downwards. Since forces result from mutual interactions, the air must also be pushing the bird upwards. The size of the force on the air equals the size of the force on the bird; the direction of the force on the air (downwards) is opposite the direction of the force on the bird (upwards). For every action, there is an equal (in size) and opposite (in direction) reaction. Action-reaction force pairs make it possible for birds to fly.

Given the facts regarding Sir Isaac Newton's third law of motion, this simple law of physics allows me to prove my bases for a new Law of Motion, the Law of Sacrifice. The word sacrifice can be used as a noun or a verb. In the application of the Law of Sacrifice, we use the word sacrifice as a noun.

We define sacrifice as the act of giving up something highly valued for the sake of something else considered to have greater value or claim. Sacrifice does not mean giving up something for nothing. It means giving up one thing for something else we believe is worth more.

Therefore, the Law of Sacrifice states that success in life's aspirations are inextricably related to personal sacrifice. You cannot get something you want without giving up something in return. In order to attain something you believe is of greater value, you must give up something you believe is of great value. Although the Law of Sacrifice utilizes physical science principles, such as Newton's 3rd Law, it is not based fully on these finite set of parameters.

The Law of Sacrifice is a divine principle. It operates beyond space and time and knows no limits. In its most pure and noble form, the Law of Sacrifice is based on the Theology of Retribution, which is you reap what you sow.

Consider aspiring to be wealthy as an example.

Understanding the law of sacrifice, you will have to decide to give something away for you to receive wealth. Therefore, reaching your goals may mean you have to sacrifice a person or a group of people in order for you to reach your desired end. You may also give your time, effort, energy, financial resources and value creation for you to receive wealth in return.

The Law of Sacrifice does not suggest that accomplishing your goals will be easy if you follow the rules. Nor is there a rational exchange for input of time for output of results. However, it does state that if you endure your race, in the fullness of time, you will accomplish your goal.

The fullness of time does not mean that it will happen if you wait long enough. The fullness of time means there is a process of maturation you must go through that will prepare you to receive the blessing you are seeking. Although time is an integral part of this process, it is not the only factor.

Therefore, if you want to become wealthy and take shortcuts to obtain wealth, you will suffer consequences. For example, if you steal, find or win money, because you disobey the Law of Sacrifice and receive something without properly paying for it, you have a debt that you owe.

Debts always have to be repaid. In the fullness of time, you may have to repay such debt by experiencing extreme family problems centered around the money, you may come to the understanding that wealth was not something you really wanted or it did not fulfill you. Finally, you may lose wealth because you were not properly prepared to receive the blessing.

As you apply the Law of Sacrifice, know that letting go of a person, circumstance or group of people is exerting an energy of sacrifice that pushes those lesser values impeding progress towards your goals out of your way. At the same time, God is pushing towards you, with equal force, the right person, circumstance or group of people that will help you achieve your goals and help you realize your purpose.

ABOUT THE AUTHOR

As the President and CEO of Serenity Village Inc, Serenity Village Insurance & Consulting and Sweet Talk Wireless, Gary Hartfield is passionate about bettering his community and sharing his experiences to inspire others. He began his career in higher education and then decided to pursue an MBA in business which he earned from the University of West Florida in 1999. He left his pursuit of a career in higher education to attend to his passion for business.

His compassion for others led him to launch Serenity Village Inc., which consists of several assisted living communities in Florida, and Serenity Village Insurance and Consulting, LLC. He has since gone on to invest in and launch several startups, one of which is Sweet Talk Wireless. His business acumen has helped him turn his ideas and passions into reality, and grow his businesses and their success.

The Entrepreneur's Publisher

RICHTER
PUBLISHING